W9-AGC-332

FAMILY TIME

St. Louis de Montfort
11441 Hague Rd.
Fishers, IN 46038

FAMILY TIME

101 Great Ideas for Sunday Afternoons

Debbie Trafton O'Neal

DIMENSIONS

FOR LIVING

NASHVILLE

FAMILY TIME
101 GREAT IDEAS FOR SUNDAY AFTERNOONS

Copyright © 1994 by Dimensions for Living

All rights reserved.
No part of this work may be reproduced or transmitted in any form or by any means, electronic or mechanical, including photocopying and recording, or by any information storage or retrieval system, except as may be expressly permitted by the 1976 Copyright Act or in writing from the publisher. Requests for permission should be addressed to Dimensions for Living, 201 Eighth Avenue South, P.O. Box 801, Nashville TN 37202.

This book is printed on acid-free, recycled paper.

Library of Congress Cataloging-in-Publication Data

O'NEAL, DEBBIE TRAFTON.
    Family time:101 great ideas for Sunday afternoons/
Debbie Trafton O'Neal.
        p. cm.
    ISBN 0-687-38507-5
    1. Family recreation. 2. Amusements. I. Title.
GV182.8.O54   1994
790.1'91—dc20   93-5065
                                                            CIP

Scripture quotations are from the *Holy Bible, New International Version.* Copyright © 1973, 1978, 1984 International Bible Society. Used by permission of Zondervan Publishing House. All rights reserved.

94 95 96 97 98 99 00 01 02 03 — 10 9 8 7 6 5 4 3 2 1

MANUFACTURED IN THE UNITED STATES OF AMERICA

To families—our circles of love

Contents

MAY DAYS

JUNE DAYS

JULY DAYS

AUGUST DAYS

SEPTEMBER DAYS

OCTOBER DAYS

NOVEMBER DAYS

DECEMBER DAYS

Introduction

*W*elcome to *Family Time*—time to make the memories that your children will look back on as some of the best times in their lives.

Although current research and statistics (as well as good old common sense!) tell us that time spent together as a family is time well spent, it can be daunting to carve out such daily time in our fast-paced world. The time I'm talking about is not the time spent gathering belongings to dash out the door, or the shuffling of kids from one activity to another. Of course, sometimes these too can be great times! But the time I'm talking about is the intentional time spent together as a family. This book suggests that Sunday afternoons are an ideal time to plan for "family time."

Why Sunday afternoons? The times we live in often seem chaotic—many parents and children echo a refrain about life being like a merry-go-round that doesn't slow down. Parents today, although always looking to the future, are also beginning to remember the past. They want to reclaim some of the traditions of "good old-fashioned" Sundays as a way to strengthen their family ties today.

The importance of the sabbath as a day of rest for all creation is taking on new meaning for many families. With scheduled activities and responsibilities from Monday through Saturday, Sunday afternoon seems to be one of the preferred times for family members to relax and enjoy one another. Just as we set aside time to start a Sunday morning with worship, so it is important for us to set aside regular time to enjoy the gift of our family.

This book is full of ideas for every Sunday afternoon of the year—and then some! Use it through many years, going straight through and back again, or pick and choose only the kind of things you would like to do.

There are games to play, suggestions of books to read, excursions to take, things to make, and experiments to try. I have attempted to include something for everyone, knowing full well that not all families would look for the same things in their Sunday afternoon adventures.

There is such a variety of things to do and try that at times you may be unsure of an activity's age-appropriateness for your child or children. It is my intent that this book be a resource for all ages, and for that reason I have not specified age-level restrictions on activities and outings. As you are choosing activities from *Family Time*, please keep in mind that children grow and develop at different rates. You are your own best judge of the kinds of Sunday afternoon events your family will be interested in and able to handle successfully. Remember, if there is a great idea that you feel your children just aren't ready for, save that idea for another time!

Although this book is written primarily for individual families, some activities suggest inviting other families, friends, or neighbors to join in. Try this! When talking with families about what helped their children become mature, responsible adults, most have told me that they had family friends—that is, that entire families were friends with one another.

I believe that God created us to enjoy the world and the people in it. It is my hope that these activities will help you and your family to do just that. You will find appropriate Bible references sprinkled throughout these pages; I hope you also will find the Spirit of God moving through these suggestions of ways for you and your family to love and laugh together on Sunday afternoons!

FAMILY TIME

JANUARY DAYS

*T*here is something exciting about the beginning of a new year, when the calendar pages are empty and dreams and goals are fresh and new. For families with children, September may seem more like the beginning of a new year because, traditionally, school has started in the fall. But as times change, many school districts have begun to use a different type of yearly calendar, so any month could be thought of as a new beginning.

Through ages past, the promise of spring has always been a time of cleaning, freshening up, and looking ahead to longer, warmer days. It is the same today.

Different and interesting traditions have sprung up in many cultures. In the United States, January 1 is the traditional New Year's Day. Parties and celebrations, as well as the traditional football games, take place both on the eve of New Year's Day and on the day itself. As you and your family begin to explore some new and different things to do, you may be starting your own family traditions for the holiday!

THIS NEW YEAR

1. Family Calendar

You will need: a large wall calendar; colorful felt-tip pens or stickers.

Busy families are looking for ways to reclaim family time. Sunday afternoons are a wonderful place to start, and making a family calendar for each month is a good way to make sure that family moments happen every day.

Purchase or make a large wall calendar. If you make your own, write the dates in the appropriate spaces. Then add the events or appointments that happen regularly, such as piano lessons or sport practices. Use stickers, or draw small pictures to designate special events—perhaps a soccer tournament or a doctor's appointment.

In addition to these scheduled events, be sure to add major cleaning or household chores such as washing and vacuuming out the car, bathing the dog, or cleaning out a toy box, as well as "just-for-fun" activities. Include some activities in which everyone in the family, even the youngest, can participate.

2. New Year Time Capsule

You will need: a box or container; tape; paper; felt-tip pens; family photos; other mementos, such as a current weekly magazine, newspaper, or schoolwork samples

It is fun to make a family time capsule that you can "dig up" next New Year's Day to review the past year by looking at family or school photos, samples of schoolwork, and other mementos of interest.

Give everyone a piece of paper to write down their hopes, dreams, and resolutions, as well as three ways they think they may change by the next year. The adults in the family can help the non-writing children complete their lists. Then carefully pack all mementos you have chosen, along with everyone's lists, in the container and seal it, to be opened next year!

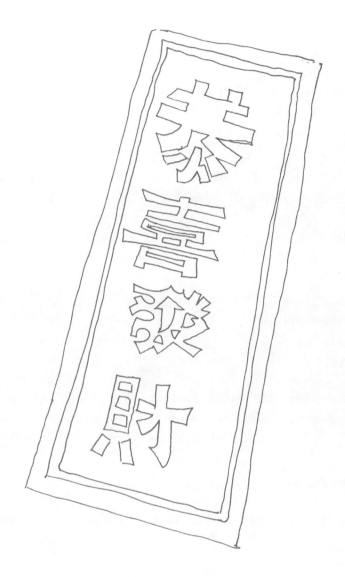

3. Chinese New Year Fun

You will need: red paper; black felt-tip pens or paint; assorted colors of construction paper; recipe ingredients for "Sweet Year Cake."

The Chinese New Year includes many days of feasting and celebration, culminating with a parade that usually includes the longest paper dragon you've ever seen! If you live in an area that has an oriental population, take advantage of the many special meals and events during this celebration. And here are a few ideas of some other things to do.

Red is a traditional color of joy and celebration in China. Use red construction paper to make bookmarks for everyone in your family. Follow the diagram of the Chinese characters and write them on your bookmarks. These words (loosely translated) mean "New Year's luck and greetings." The characters are pronounced "gon she fa tsi."

This recipe is for a cake usually eaten for breakfast on the actual first day of the Chinese New Year. It tastes great!

SWEET YEAR CAKE

1 pound glutinous rice flour
3 eggs
3 cups milk
1 to 1½ cups sugar
¾ stick margarine

Mix ingredients together well. Pour into a glass baking dish and bake at 375° for 30 to 40 minutes.

4. A Worthy Life

As the new year begins, it is time to take stock of who we are as people of God. Every day brings challenges that test our faith, and even our attitudes toward the people we live and work with. This is a good time to reflect on the words of Paul in Ephesians, as we strive to be worthy of God's call to us. Use this verse as the basis of family thought, prayer, and discussion, perhaps helping everyone to memorize and put into practice its key principles.

> I urge you to live a life worthy of the calling you have received. Be completely humble and gentle; be patient, bearing with one another in love. Make every effort to keep the unity of the Spirit through the bond of peace. (Eph. 4:1b-3)

SNOWY WEATHER

If you live in a part of the country that has wonderful winter weather, or if you have only a short distance to travel to find snow, you can have a great Sunday afternoon playing together! Just be sure to dress warmly and take breaks for food and water—all that exercise in the cold air can deplete your energy supply quickly! And of course, a thermos or pot of hot cocoa, and warm, dry socks are a nice plus!

Whatever you do in the snow, stop to notice the quiet wonder of the white blanket that covers the ground. There is nothing quite like a fresh snowfall and the quiet of the world hushed after a snowstorm to make us realize how great our God is! Sometimes, if you are very quiet, you can even hear the snowflakes as they fall to the ground!

It is at times like this that I believe God is speaking to us with the words from Psalm 46:10*a*: "Be still, and know that I am God."

5. Snow Play

You will need: a patch of clean snow

It is so much fun to make snow angels! Show your children how to lie on their backs in the snow, spread their arms, and swish them back and forth from shoulder to head to make the angel's wings. Swishing their legs back and forth will make the angel's robe. Carefully help one another up. How many angels can your family make?

Another fun thing to do in the snow is to make a snow sculpture or igloo. Of course, a snowperson with all the traditional trimmings is nice, but what about making a snow dinosaur or bear or alligator?

A snow fort is easy to make by packing snow together, but it is fun to make a real igloo-type structure by packing snow into a small bowl or pan to make a snow brick. Plop each brick out, then stack them up to form the wall. Alternate the bricks, leaving gaps and spaces as you work. When your igloo is built, whether it is large or small, it is fun to light a candle or two to set inside in the center space. (Be sure to put the candle in a glass candle holder or small bowl for safety.) When you step back and look, your igloo will be a shining ice sculpture in your front yard!

What if it snows at your house, but someone is sick and can't go outside to join in the fun? Well, just bring the snow to them!

Fill a bucket with snow and bring it in your house. Dump the snow either in the kitchen sink or in the bathtub, where it is easy to play with cups, measuring spoons, and bowls. Build snow sculptures inside the sink or tub, and when the fun is done, just pull the plug! The melted snow will go right down the drain.

Before you leave your snow field, whether it is in your front yard or up in the mountains, save a bit of winter for one of the hot summer afternoons sure to come. Let every family member make a snowball and put it into a zip-type plastic bag. Remove the excess air and seal the bag, then put it into the freezer. (If you are away from home, take along an insulated or styrofoam cooler to keep the snowballs cold for the trip home.)

> **"Be still, and know that I am God." (Psalm 46:10a)**

KITCHEN GARDENING

Did you know that even in the midst of winter, there is a great source for a garden growing in your grocery store? A green thumb is something that seems to come naturally to children, and they are amazed and astonished by the way a plant can grow from a tiny seed. Of course, a trip to a hothouse nursery in the cold of winter is fun, but the adventure of growing your own kitchen garden makes springtime seem nearer.

6. Everything Is Sprouting

You will need: a new sponge; garden cress or alfalfa seeds; a shallow dish; water; scissors.

The seeds of alfalfa or garden cress are quick to sprout and great to eat! You can add your harvest to sandwiches and salads, or just eat it plain.

To start with, you will need to rinse your new sponge several times in clear, cold water. Wring the sponge out after the final rinse and place it in a shallow dish. Sprinkle your seeds on the sponge and add water to the dish.

By the next day, the seeds will already begin to crack open. By the third day, you may be able to see the roots, and if you have "planted" garden cress, the leaves will begin to form by the fifth day.

In less than two weeks, you can snip your harvest and eat it!

7. Fruit and Vegetable Seeds

You will need: any fruit or vegetable seeds or pits that you would like to plant (such as a piece of sweet potato, an avocado pit, seeds from an apple, orange, lemon, grapefruit, or pumpkin); jars or paper cups; toothpicks; water; soil (additional items: shallow dish or saucer, pebbles, carrot or pineapple tops, sand and coffee grounds, plastic bag, apple pieces)

A sweet potato or an avocado pit can grow in water. Fill a jar with clean water and attach toothpicks to the potato or avocado as shown, so that the top stays above the water. Add enough water so that the bottom of the pit or potato is always covered. Keep the jar in a sunny place and watch the roots grow down as the leaves grow up. Don't give up if it seems to take a while!

Other fruit and vegetable seeds, such as apple seeds, are easy to grow in a cup. Fill the cup with soil and plant the seeds near the top, covering them lightly with the soil. Place the seeds in a sunny place and water each day. How long before the seeds begin to grow?

Other fun things to try growing in your kitchen garden are carrot or pineapple tops. Carrot tops with a small amount of green on them can be placed in a saucer with water, between small pebbles. The leafy tops will soon grow bigger and bigger.

If you ever have a pineapple, cut off the top, leaving about an inch of the fruit still attached, and let it dry in the air for a day or so. Then spread a layer of pebbles on the bottom of a shallow dish and add a layer of moist soil, mixed with sand and coffee grounds. Set the pineapple top in the center of the dish and cover the fruit part with more soil, so that only the leaves show above the soil line. Pat down the soil and water it well.

Keep the pot in a warm and sunny spot like a kitchen window, making sure that the soil is moist but not too soggy. Pour the water right into the leaves of the plant when you water it. A pineapple is a bromeliad, and bromeliads take in water through their leaves. Be patient! Even though it didn't take long to eat or plant your pineapple, it can take several months before new green shoots start coming out through the crown of leaves.

If you would like to see if your pineapple plant can make a flower and perhaps a baby pineapple, put a few pieces of cut-up apple into the soil and slip a plastic bag over the top of the plant. Fasten it shut and leave it for four or five days. The apple will give off ethylene gas and might encourage the plant to make a flower and baby pineapple!

8. Can a Corn Plant Grow from a Kernel of Popcorn?

You will need: popcorn kernels; zip-type plastic bag; soil, water; suction-cup hook or tape; a sunny window

Do you think you can grow a small corn plant from a popcorn kernel? You can! Everyone is amazed with this fun kitchen-garden project.

Place several spoonfuls of potting soil in a plastic bag, and then push one or two kernels of popcorn into the soil. Water lightly and zip the bag closed so that the inside of the bag becomes like a terrarium.

Hang the plastic bag in a sunny window using a suction-cup hook or a piece of tape. Write the date on a piece of tape and attach it to the bag. Later, when you first see the roots and leaves begin to form, add another piece of tape with that day's date. How many days did it take?

FEBRUARY DAYS

February, the shortest month of the year, offers Sundays that can be cold and dreary—the perfect time for some family fun! Whether you choose to spend a Sunday afternoon on the town or snuggled up by the fire with a good book, there should be plenty of choices here for you and your family.

TOWN AND COUNTRY

9. City Walking Tour

You will need: a book or other information about different kinds of architecture (especially those that are unique to your area); a town or city map; a sketchbook or pad and pencil for each family member

A walking tour of your own city or town, or a particularly interesting nearby city or town, is a great way to spend a Sunday afternoon. If the weather is cold, be sure to bundle up!

Before you start on your walk, read and talk about the basic kinds of architecture you might find. These will vary, depending upon which part of the country you live in, but the older and most unique styles usually will be found in the downtown areas. Use the map to plan your route, taking into consideration how far your youngest family members can walk and the location of good resting points.

If there are designated historic homes and buildings in your town, this is a good place to begin. As you walk, point out differences in the streets—for example, some portions might be brick or cobblestone, and then change to concrete as you walk farther on. Notice the different types of chimneys and roofs, and buildings with bricked-over windows.

Encourage everyone to try sketching buildings or parts of buildings that they particularly like.

When you arrive home, take time to share everyone's sketches and frame those that you especially like to hang in your home as a reminder of your Sunday afternoon city-sights excursion.

To adapt this excursion to a country setting, prepare by gathering information about the wildlife and vegetation you may see on your walk.

10. Town or Country Scavenger Hunt

You will need: your car; a list of things to look for

Turn a Sunday afternoon drive into a family scavenger hunt! Make a list of things to look for as you drive, such as:

- an ice-cream-cone stand or a store that sells ice-cream cones
- a house painted three colors
- a tree swing
- a cow
- a building more than 100 years old
- a dirt road
- a cemetery
- a church
- a lake or pond
- a street with the name of a person
- a tree with red berries (and so on)

Naturally, you will need to create your own list, based on the area where you will be driving. Of course, it would be nice to end your Sunday afternoon scavenger hunt at a little place for a bite to eat, or at least an ice-cream cone!

BOOKWORKS

There is nothing quite like a good book when the cold winds begin to blow! Research shows that children who are read to become better readers. What better reason than that for reading aloud together as a family?

11. Family Book List

You will need: access to a good children's bookstore or library; a notebook; pen or pencil

Family reading time is a tradition in nearly every family, whether it is a nightly bedtime story or a Bible story every Sunday. Why not begin a notebook of family favorites, or books your family would like to read, complete with the comments and thoughts your family shares after reading them? Your notebook that chronicles family reading can become a treasury of times well-spent with books that help us to travel the world over.

Books that offer reading lists for specific age groups or certain areas of interest are available. Check with your librarian or a bookstore to find such a resource to get you started.

Of course, a good place to begin is with the books you knew and loved as a child, including favorite fairytales and legends, as well as Bible stories and storybooks. Some great possibilities include C. S. Lewis's *Chronicles of Narnia, The Boxcar Children* by Gertrude Chandler, and of course, the *Little House on the Prairie* books by Laura Ingalls Wilder.

The *Winnie the Pooh* books by A. A. Milne are treasured by children and adults of all ages. A special Pooh cookbook that includes honey cakes and other such yummies accompanies some versions of these favorite stories. A cookbook volume is available with *The Little House on the Prairie* books as well.

There are many new books for beginning readers within the Christian market. Some of these are retellings of Bible stories, while others are contemporary tales with a Christian emphasis. Check with a local Christian bookstore for the latest releases.

Many good Bible storybooks are now available as well, including my book, *My Read-and-Do Bible Storybook*, appropriate for families with children in a broad age range. Not only does it include stories from both the Old and New Testaments, but it also incorporates the philosophy that children learn best by doing and by experience. Every Bible story includes verses, prayers, and "things to do" that reinforce the Bible story in a meaningful way.

Other good Bible storybooks include *The Early Reader's Bible* and *The Beginner's Bible*. Of course, there are many more to choose from, depending upon the age of your child.

Check for new and different versions of individual Bible stories as well, especially those that are illustrated in different ways. Everyone appreciates picture books with a new angle or twist!

And don't forget that reading the Bible together is important, even if you feel that the language may not be written at your child's level. It is especially good to read a portion of the Bible verse, or an entire story with which your family is very familiar, and then talk together about what it means for us today.

One of the greatest gifts parents can give children is their time. Reading together is one of the best ways I know to do this. When my children were old enough, I found simplified versions of *Robinson Crusoe, Tom Sawyer,* and many of Shakespeare's works to read aloud. Try to include some such priceless gifts as these for your children. Remember, a book read early may stimulate interest in a specific topic that may turn into new hobby or interest.

A good verse to keep in mind as you choose books for your family is found in Proverbs: "Apply your heart to instruction and your ears to words of knowledge" (23:12). Is there any better counsel to encourage parents and children to read together?

12. Book Quilt

You will need: white paper; fabric crayons or acrylic paints; an iron; muslin or another plain fabric, cut into 10-inch squares; quilt batting; sewing machine and thread

Ask everyone in the family to choose a favorite part of a book you have read recently, and then use fabric crayons to draw a picture of it on a sheet of white paper. Make sure the pictures are colored heavily. Then follow the directions on the crayons to transfer the color to a piece of fabric; this usually involves using an iron. When all the pictures have been transferred, set them aside until you are ready to sew all the squares together to make your quilt.

As you and your family continue to read, make other quilt squares. When you have enough squares of favorite parts of books to make a good-sized quilt, sew the squares together and finish with quilt batting. This will be a wonderful keepsake to treasure through the years!

A LOVING SUNDAY

Valentine's Day is one of schoolchildren's favorite holidays, and—let's face it—it's one that adults who love flowers, hearts, and chocolates love to celebrate as well! As children of God, we are loved each day, but it's fun to make a Sunday afternoon extra-special by celebrating that love with our families.

Plan a party for your family's afternoon and evening. During or right after lunch, plan and then prepare the food and decorations for an evening meal. Some of the following ideas may start your family's new tradition of honoring loved ones during the whole month of February, as well as on Sunday afternoons. Try any ideas that appeal to you, and add others of your own!

13. Red Day

You will need: everything red—your clothes; funny socks; hair ribbons; placemats; dishes; food; balloons—also, scissors; and so on

Decorate your house with red balloons, crepe paper streamers, and decorations of all kinds to celebrate this day of loving. Be sure everyone in the family has at least one red item to wear. Make red paper hearts, if you don't have red clothing items.

If you don't have a red tablecloth or placemats, you can make placemats as one of your activities. Have fun scalloping or zig-zagging the edges of construction paper, or weave placemats by cutting slits in the paper and alternating strips of other colors. Of course, you will need to cut out lots and lots of red hearts to decorate the room as well.

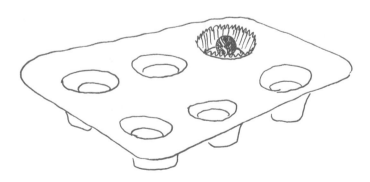

Brainstorm together with your family to think of red foods that you could combine to make your meal festive. How about red punch? Red gelatin cut into heart shapes? Pink cupcakes, or a cake with red candies? Red apple wedges? The possibilities are endless.

Here's a simple way to make heart-shaped cupcakes. Fill a muffin pan with paper muffin cups; then place a glass marble or small ball of foil into each cup, between the paper and one side of the cup. When you pour the cupcake batter in, the marble will help to make the heart shape. Be sure you don't fill the muffin cups too full, or you will lose the heart shape.

14. Lacing Hearts

You will need: wallpaper scraps; construction paper or colored posterboard; adhesive-backed clear vinyl; heavy clear plastic (available at most fabric stores); scissors; yarn; hole punch for paper; small candies or toys

Draw a heart on a 6-inch square of paper of your choice. Then cut a 6-inch square of clear adhesive vinyl, remove the backing, lay the adhesive over the paper, and cut out the heart shape. Then cut the same size heart from the clear plastic.

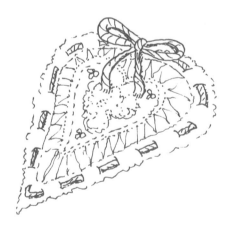

Place the clear plastic heart and the paper heart together, with the vinyl on top. Use the paper punch to make holes around both heart pieces, trying to keep the edges spaced evenly and the same distance from the edge. Hold the hearts together tightly to keep them from sliding.

To lace the hearts together, place the clear plastic heart on top, making sure the holes line up. Cut a 36-inch piece of yarn and begin lacing the pieces together by pulling the yarn through the holes, beginning at the top of the heart.

When you've laced around the bottom of the heart, fill the heart with small candies or the other items you have chosen, then continue lacing. When you reach the top, use the remaining yarn to tie a bow to keep the heart closed. Share your laced hearts with someone you love!

> Create in me a pure heart, O God,
> and renew a steadfast spirit within me.
> (Psalm 51:10)

EASTER IS COMING

The season of Lent (the six weeks prior to Easter) is one of the great times during the Christian year. It is at this time that God's people begin to think about the great gift of new life. Use your Sunday afternoon together to reflect upon the gifts in your own family's life.

15. Plan a Celebration

You will need: party supplies; decorations and food; invitations (if you would like to have friends or other families celebrate with you)

Originally, the season of Lent began with a festive celebration so that people could dispose of their rich and fatty foods before the austere Lenten season of fasting and penitence. For many families, this meant combining their eggs, butter, and other rich foods into pancakes, cakes, and other goodies.

You and your family can create your own celebration, using the party foods and decorations you have on hand. Popcorn is always fun, as well as chips and dips, ice cream, and all your other family favorites.

Plan games and music for your party, including some traditional games such as musical chairs, hot potato, and pin the tail on the donkey. A balloon-sitting contest is fun, as are wheelbarrow races and three-legged races. The sky's the limit when planning your party!

16. A Basket of Easter

You will need: a basket; plastic bag; potting soil; grass seed

If you begin growing this basket of grass now, it should be ready to hide eggs in on Easter Sunday!

Cut the plastic bag to fit inside the basket. Mix the soil with a very small amount of water to dampen it, and spoon the damp soil into the bag. Make sure you leave an edge of the plastic bag hanging out over the edge of the basket; this can be trimmed off later.

Sprinkle a thin layer of grass seed on top of the soil. To speed up germination, place the basket in a warm, well-lit window and keep the soil moist by watering or misting gently every day. As your grass begins to grow, you can give it a haircut with scissors if it gets too long!

MARCH DAYS

"I n like a lion, out like a lamb"—so the saying goes. The month of March is known for turbulent and often unpredictable weather, which makes it hard to plan on certain types of weather-related activities and outings. Of course, when there is wind, it is a perfect time for kite-making and kite-flying. And doesn't rain make the fish bite?

WHEN THE WIND BLOWS

Have fun in the windy days of March! If possible, rent or borrow the videotape of *Mary Poppins*, who blew in and out when the wind changed. Most people are not familiar with the many other books about Mary Poppins, written by P. L. Travers. If you and your family are reading together, March is a great month to read more about Mary Poppins and her adventures. Here are a few "wind adventures" for your own family to try!

17. Paper-bag Kite or Windsock

You will need: a large paper bag; string; hole punch for paper and hole reinforcements; scraps of tissue paper and crepe paper; glue; paints or felt-tip pens; string or yarn

To make your paper-bag kite, fold the open edge of the paper bag in about 2 inches for strength. Punch a hole in each of the four corners of the bag at least 1 inch from the folded edge, and attach a reinforcement to each hole.

Cut four strings and tie each through a hole, making knots inside the bag. Bring the strings together in the middle and tie them in a knot, making a loop with the four ends for a handle, as shown. Paint or decorate the bag with glue and tissue-paper scraps. Cut crepe-paper streamers and attach to the bottom edge of the bag. After the glue is dry, open the bag, hold on to the string, and run so that the wind catches in the bag and makes the kite fly.

To adapt this paper bag for a windsock, cut the bottom out of the bag and fold in both the bottom and top edges of the bag about 2 inches. Follow the directions for the holes and string given above. Decorate as you like, attaching streamers to the bottom of the bag. When dry, hang your completed windsock from a hook or tree in your yard. Watch the streamers dance in the wind!

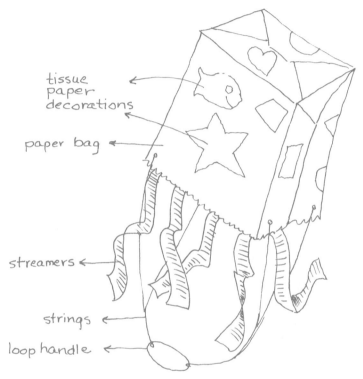

tissue paper decorations

paper bag

streamers

strings

loop handle

18. Blow, Pinwheel, Blow

You will need: one square of construction or wrapping paper, approximately 10 inches in diameter; scissors; a new pencil with an eraser on top; a straight pin or tack

Make a simple pinwheel for each person in your family! Draw intersecting diagonal lines on the paper square as shown, making a circle in the center. Help the youngest children cut the lines to the center circle. Then hold the pieces together in the center with one hand and bend the paper toward the center, being careful not to crease it. When all the pieces are turned toward the center in pinwheel fashion, carefully push a straight pin or tack through the paper and into the eraser on the end of the pencil. Leave a little space between the paper and the eraser to make it easier for the wind to blow the pinwheel.

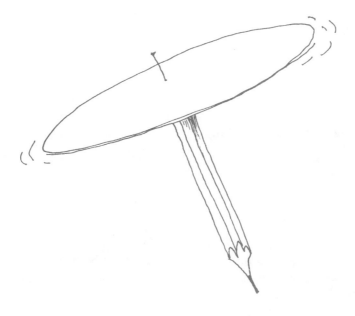

19. Clouds Rolling By

You will need: time; a hillside; a breezy day; clouds in the sky

For centuries, farmers and navigators have watched the sky for guidance in their planting and harvests, and in their travels. Cloud-watching makes a Sunday afternoon a memorable experience, a time to relax before the Monday-morning rush.

Find a grassy hillside or field to lie down in (be sure to ask permission if you are on private property!), and point out the shapes of things you can see in the sky. Once you begin spotting castles and dragons and horses, children begin to see them as well.

There is something so enjoyable about watching the clouds roll by. Perhaps it is just a reminder of a simpler time, when responsibilities were few. Or perhaps it reminds us that the world is so much bigger than our small corner, and it is good that God is in charge. Whatever the case, it is true that once your children have seen pictures in the clouds, they will always look at clouds differently from the way other people do.

If you have the opportunity to watch the wind blowing the clouds around, why not tell your family the story found in John 6:16-21? In that passage, evening has fallen, and the disciples have entered a boat to cross the lake for Capernaum. But as darkness falls, Jesus is not with them. Then a strong wind comes up and the water of the lake becomes rough. In their terror, the disciples begin to row as rapidly as possible to reach the shore. Suddenly, they see Jesus walking on the water toward them, and he says to them, "Don't be afraid—it is I." And only when they have taken Jesus into the boat with them do they cease their trembling.

After retelling this story and talking about it together, share your thoughts about times when Jesus has comforted you when you have been afraid. A few minutes of quiet reflection on a hillside can produce a growing trust and faith in God, even as the clouds roll by!

THE FISH ARE BITING

Does rainy weather make the fish bite? How hard is it to bait a worm on a hook? These questions and more, including stories about "the big one that got away," make a great theme for a Sunday afternoon. These "fishing fun" activities can take place inside or out.

20. Fish Pond

You will need: a broomstick or dowel; string; magnet; fish shapes cut from paper scraps; paper clips

Attach a long string to a dowel or broomstick and tie a magnet at the end of the string. Slide the paper clips onto the paper fish, and place the fish in a "pond" (one side of a couch or table).

To fish, have family members lean over the back of the couch or table with the pole and try to catch fish with the magnet on the end of the string. The player who nabs the most fish wins.

Other variations on this game include numbering several fish and adding them up, color-coding the fish and trying to catch only fish of a certain color, or writing questions on each fish and instructing the fisherpeople to answer the questions in order to keep their catch. Think up other variations of your own!

Nothing can quite compare with the taste of fresh fish, though, so make sure that a fishing trip of some sort is on your list of Sunday afternoon excursions. Depending upon whether you fish from a bridge, a dock, or a boat, and the part of the country in which you live, your fishing experience will be different from that of every other family.

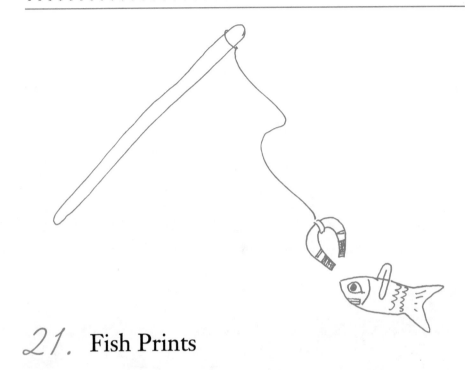

21. Fish Prints

You will need: a fresh fish (perhaps one you have caught); paper towels; printing ink; a printing roller (brayer); a baking sheet covered with aluminum foil; paper or white T-shirts

When you catch a fish you particularly like, or if you can find a whole fish at a fish market or grocery store, make a print of it to prove that this one really didn't get away!

Wash and dry the fish by blotting with paper towels. Squeeze the printing ink onto the foil-covered baking sheet and roll it out with the brayer, making it smooth enough to cover the entire roller. Then roll the ink over the fish, making sure to cover it entirely.

To print the fish, you can press the paper or T-shirt onto the fish, molding it around the fish body to get a complete print. Or you can lift and turn the fish over on the paper or T-shirt, pressing it down on all edges so that the print will be complete.

Let the print dry completely and either frame or wear your catch!

> "Come, follow me," Jesus said, "and I will make you fishers of men." At once they left their nets and followed him.
>
> (Mark 1:17-18)

GAME DAY

A Sunday afternoon of popcorn and games makes for a fun family-building time. Think about all the great games you played during your own child-hood, and ask your kids about some of the games they and their friends are playing today. You might find that the games are essentially the same, that only the names have changed!

22. I Spy

To play "I Spy," the person who is "it" offers clues to guide the others in guessing what "it" sees. This is a great game for younger children because it tests their listening and observation skills.

For example, "it" says, "I spy something that is round and red, and you can eat it." When someone guesses "apple," it is his or her turn to be "it."

This can be a great game to play while taking a Sunday afternoon drive, no matter where you are going.

23. Silly Sally

To play "Silly Sally," the person who is the leader says, "Silly Sally likes *something*, but not *something*." For example, "Silly Sally likes puppies but not dogs," or "Silly Sally likes boots but not shoes," or "Silly Sally likes pizza but not tacos."

Have you figured out what Silly Sally likes? Silly Sally likes things that have double letters in them! Of course, it is easier to figure out what Silly Sally likes if you can write down the things Silly Sally likes and notice the pattern, but this game offers older players a great opportunity to use their listening and reasoning skills.

24. Memory Tray

You will need: a tray; assorted objects, such as a comb, pencil, quarter, small toy, and so on; a scarf or towel

Depending upon the ages of the children in your family, you will want to limit the number of items you place on the memory tray at one time. After placing several items on the tray, let everyone take a good look at the tray; then cover it with the scarf or towel.

Now ask each family member to name the items he or she saw on the tray. Who remembered the most? As you play this game again and again, changing the number of items or using a variety of different items each time, everyone in your family will become better and better at remembering what was on the tray. Another great observation game!

APRIL DAYS

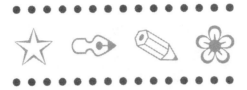

S howers, rain, flowers, bunnies, eggs, the cross—April is one of the months we look forward to all year—the month of new life and new beginnings. Easter Sunday, the best beginning of all, usually falls in April, although it can fall in March, depending upon the calendar.

But whenever Easter Sunday arrives, it is indeed a special Sunday to celebrate with your family. You may have tried some of the ideas suggested here, and you also may have other family traditions that are significant to you. Whatever you decide to do on Easter Sunday, do it joyfully and together!

EASTER IS HERE!

Here are some things to try when you and your family celebrate Easter Sunday together.

25. Easter Basket

You will need: the basket of grass you "planted" in February, or another basket with artificial Easter grass; candy and hard-boiled eggs; a small chick or rabbit figure, or any other items you may wish to place in the basket

Decorate your Easter basket by adding the candy or hard-boiled eggs. Then insert several small figures of animals or chicks so that they seem to be hiding in the grass. Use this basket to nibble from during the afternoon and as a centerpiece at your evening meal.

26. Easter-egg Tree

You will need: a sturdy tree branch with smaller branches extending out from it; coffee can; white spray paint; decorated blown or plastic eggs; paper and scissors; ribbons; florist's foam or plaster of paris

Decorate the coffee can with paint and spray the branch white. To stabilize the branch in the can, fit the florist's foam into the bottom of the can, or if you are using plaster of paris, follow the directions on the package.

When the branch is steady, tie ribbons on the eggs you have decorated or collected, and hang them from the branches of your Easter tree. Make this Easter tree special by hanging crosses cut from paper on the branches as well.

Throughout the year, take time to make and decorate eggs; they can be saved and added to the tree next year.

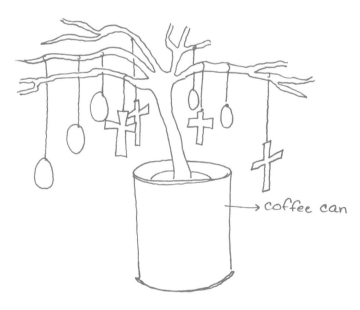

coffee can

27. Easter-egg Cans

You will need: clean empty soup cans; acrylic or spray paints; sponges; scraps of wallpaper or wrapping paper; wire; permanent felt-tip pens; small pink pom-poms; a hot-glue gun; artificial Easter grass; Easter candies; nail and hammer; Bible verses written on slips of paper; a nursing home or care facility that would welcome visitors on Easter Sunday

Using the illustration as a guide, paint the cans with white paint. When dry, sponge on pink, blue, or light green paints for a mottled effect. Let dry.

With a nail, hammer a small hole on each side at the top of each can and insert the wire. Bring the ends of the wire up high enough for a handle and twist together.

For each can, cut two rabbit ears from wallpaper and crease down the center. Glue the ears to the cans with the glue gun. Use the felt-tip pens to draw a face on the front of each can, and glue on a small pink pom-pom for each nose.

Fill the cans with the artificial grass and small candies, as well as the slips of paper with your favorite Bible verses. Take the cans to the nursing home or care facility to share with residents who may not have any other visitors on Easter Sunday.

soup can with sponge-painted spots

RAINY DAYS

Many people think of a rainy day only as an invitation to stay indoors. Not so! Depending upon the intensity of the rain, there are many fun things to do; and if you have been cooped up because of the weather all weekend, a rainy-day walk or puddle-jumping contest is just what you need to lift your spirits before the new week begins!

28. Rainy-day Walk

You will need: boots; raincoats; umbrellas; any other rainy-day gear

The world looks different when it rains! Have everyone put on their boots and coats, and take a walk together down your street. Notice the rainbows in the oily places on the road or in the parking lot. See how the earthworms come crawling out when it rains. Who can find the longest one?

What things do you find washing down the street in the water that runs into the gutter? Take along a toy boat to float down the street with you.

Teach your children the words to "Singing in the Rain," and sing it together as you walk along.

Sometimes a rainy-day walk isn't planned—it just happens. Take advantage of the opportunity to make lasting memories. After dashing inside out of the rain, peeling off wet clothes and taking warm showers, finish off with a cup of hot cocoa!

29. Rain Paintings

You will need: paper; scissors; dry tempera paints, or water colors and brushes

Have you ever wondered what designs the rain would make, if it could paint? On the next rainy Sunday, try this activity to find out.

Cut raindrop shapes from paper and take them outside during the next light rain (but not during a downpour).

Lay the paper raindrop shapes on the sidewalk and sprinkle dry tempera paints on top, or swirl watercolor paints around on them as the rain is coming down. If you use tempera, you will need to leave them outside and wait to see what they will look like when the rain stops. If you use watercolors, you can see immediate results, and when you are pleased with the design the rain has made, you can take the raindrop inside.

Let the rain paintings dry and hang them in your home.

SPRING HAS SPRUNG

Ah, springtime! A Sunday afternoon in the spring is one that beckons to families to come outside and enjoy the creation that God has made.

rain-soaked spots
on
tempera-painted
papers

All the psalms remind us of the wonders of the world God has made. Especially in the spring, it seems that the psalms speak to us clearly. The words in Psalm 121, especially in the first verse, have always been some of my favorites: "I lift up my eyes to the hills—where does my help come from?"

Maybe these words have always been special to me because I live in a state surrounded by mountains. But I suspect that these words really have special meaning because when I look up at the mountains, I am awed by their size and stately complexity. And I am reminded that the God who created the mountains is also the God who created me and all the creatures of the earth. It is a humbling experience.

30. Nest-building Helpers

You will need: scraps of yarn or string; strands of hair (saved from haircuts)

Birds are fun to watch in the spring as they scurry to and fro, finding wiggly worms and gathering materials to make their nests. You can help the birds on a Sunday afternoon by leaving small pieces of yarn, string, and hair in the crook of a nearby tree.

Although you won't be rewarded by seeing a nest built right before your eyes, you will be amazed by how quickly the birds notice the materials you have left for them. And who knows how soon you might see baby birds, just learning to fly and using your yard as a landing ground!

31. Make Way for Ducks!

You will need: bread scraps

Collect your dried or stale bread scraps in a bag throughout the week and take a drive or walk on Sunday afternoon to a nearby lake or pond. Then spend a lazy but rewarding afternoon feeding bread to the ducks in the pond.

And add a picnic lunch, or cookies and juice, for the hungry feeders.

32. Searching for Frog Eggs

You will need: a pond or marshy area; a jar with a lid; hammer and nail; fishbowl

Hammer a few nail holes in the jar lid to make air holes for the frog eggs. Then go to a pond or marshy area where you suspect you might find such eggs.

Frog eggs are usually found in a clear jelly-like mass, close to the water's edge and floating just below the surface. If you look closely, you can sometimes see a black dot in the center of each egg.

When you find some eggs, carefully scoop them up in your jar and fill the jar with the pond water. When you get home, carefully pour the eggs and the water into the fishbowl. It will be weeks, perhaps even a month, before the eggs actually hatch, depending, of course, upon the stage at which you found them.

When the water level in the fishbowl seems to be going down, return to the same pond to collect more water; it will contain the little green plants and bugs that the tadpole eggs need in order to grow.

When the tadpoles turn into small frogs, be sure to take them back to the same area and let them go.

MUSIC MAKING

Music is a big part of our lives, whether it is a song in the shower, a goodnight lullaby, or the car radio on the way to work. Before there were televisions and CD players, and even before there were many radios in homes, family times together on Sunday afternoons and evenings often involved music. Bring back the tradition in your own family in fun and different ways! Spring is the perfect time to "make a joyful noise unto the Lord"!

33. Drinking-glass Music

You will need: about 8 jars or drinking glasses; water; spoons

Line up the jars or glasses on a table and pour water into them, varying the water level in each glass. Beginning on the left, fill the first glass nearly to the top, then tap it with a spoon to make sure it produces a clear sound. This glass will be the first note in the "do, re, mi" scale.

Add water at slightly lower levels to the remaining glasses, tapping each after you have filled it to make sure it is the next note in the "do, re, mi" sound.

After you have filled all the glasses, play up and down the scale a few times to make sure the sound is clear. Now you're ready to try playing some of the songs your family likes to sing!

34. Make a Comb Kazoo

You will need: one fine-toothed comb for each person; a piece of waxed paper or tissue paper

It is easy to make a comb kazoo! Fold the piece of waxed or tissue paper in half and wrap the comb in the fold. Now hold the comb loosely between your lips, with the teeth of the comb pointing out, and hum a tune. How does it sound?

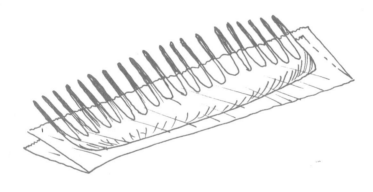

35. One-person Pole Band

You will need: a broomstick or wooden dowel; hammer and small nails; jingle bells; aluminum pie pans; other assorted "junk"

If your children are not familiar with a "one-person band," try to find a picture or example of one to show them.

Begin constructing your own family one-person pole band by experimenting with the different kinds of junk you have collected. What makes the best sound? Which could be attached to the pole with small nails or tacks to make a good sound?

When you are satisfied with the sounds made by the different portions of your pole band, hammer the nails and tacks into the pieces to make sure they are secure. Then make music and sing away, as you accompany yourself with your one-person pole band!

> "Rejoice in the Lord always. I will say it again: Rejoice!"
> (Philippians 4:4)

MAY DAYS

*T*he month of May brings the flowers that the rains of April watered! This is the month to enjoy longer days full of daylight, dust off the bikes and the baseball mitts, and get our fingers in the dirt.

Mother's Day is another holiday that always falls on a Sunday, so take advantage of that and plan something fun just for Mom!

IN THE FLOWER GARDEN

Whether you are a city or a country dweller, a small patch of dirt, even a windowbox or flowerpot, is rewarding to cultivate—especially in the springtime, when the miracle of Easter is still fresh in our minds. It is always a miracle to watch small, lifeless seeds begin to thrive and grow as we give them the proper care.

36. Flower Starts

You will need: small paper cups or empty egg cartons; potting soil; flower seeds, such as marigolds, nasturtiums, or others that germinate quickly

Fill the cups nearly to the top with soil, then press the flower seeds gently into the soil. Water lightly, place in a sunny window, and wait until the seeds become small green plants. When the plants are large enough, you can transplant them to a pot or to a flowerbed outside.

It is fun to keep a graph to show how many days it takes the seeds in each cup to begin to grow.

37. May Day Baskets

You will need: construction paper or leftover wallpaper; paper lace doilies, or white paper; scissors; tape; ribbon; flowers

Even if the first day of May doesn't fall on a Sunday, you can make May Day baskets to share with your friends and neighbors.

Roll a square of paper into a cone shape and tape along the edges so that the cone will hold its shape. Line the outer rim with doilies or lace cut from the doilies, or cut some white paper into a snowflake design and use that for the trim.

Attach a length of ribbon to the inside of the basket to make a handle. Fill the cone basket with flowers—and a note, if you want—and then deliver the baskets to your friends and neighbors in celebration of spring.

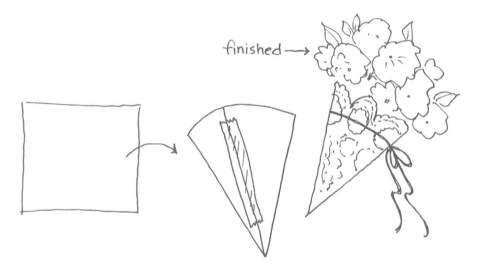

finished →

38. Pressed-flower Pictures

You will need: leaves and small spring flowers such as pansies, small ferns, and other local flowers; blotting paper or paper towels; heavy books, boxes, or boards; parchment paper; a frame; fine-tip felt pen; glue or rubber cement

Collect the small flowers and leaves that you would like to press. Arrange them on a sheet of paper, not too close together; then lay a sheet of blotting paper or a paper towel over them.

Carefully place heavy books or boards on top and leave them for about two weeks, or until the flowers are pressed flat. Then carefully lift off the paper and remove the pressed flowers.

Arrange the flowers on the sheet of parchment paper, perhaps in a heart shape, as shown. Use a small dot of glue or rubber cement to attach each flower to the paper. If you like, print its name beside or under each flower with the felt-tip pen. When dry, frame your pressed-flower art and hang it in your house.

The earth is the LORD's, and everything in it,
the world, and all who live in it.

(Psalm 24:1)

A DAY FOR MOTHERS

Mother's Day, that special day when we honor our mothers and other special women in our lives, always falls on a Sunday. Celebrating your own Mother's Day may be as simple as letting the mom in your family "have the day off," while all the other family members pitch in to cook, clean, and so on. A special bouquet of flowers and a meal are nice; a bigger party for all the mothers you know would be great too!

39. A Getaway Weekend

You will need: the entire weekend; a nearby motel or hotel with special weekend rates; whatever you would need to spend the weekend

Many motels or hotels offer special package rates around the holidays, and children always have fun doing something out of the ordinary, even if it is close to home. If you can find a motel or hotel that offers a special family rate for the weekend, perhaps with an extra bed in the room for the kids or with adjoining rooms, you can plan a fun weekend for mom that will eliminate doing dishes and making beds!

Be sure to check the prices and package arrangements, and try to find a place that offers a nice Sunday brunch for after church and a pool for everyone to enjoy in the afternoon.

40. Family Christmas Card

You will need: a camera and film; any special clothing or props you would like to include; your family

It may seem too early to think about taking a photo for a family Christmas card, but it really isn't! If you and your family have a unique hobby or interest—perhaps all of you play tennis, for example—plan to stage a few photos this Sunday that show you in action. You might want to choose several things that you and your family like to do, to share with other people this upcoming Christmas via your Christmas photo.

After you have taken several photos, have the film developed and decide which you like best. If none of them is to your satisfaction, there is still plenty of time to take more!

Mother's Day is a good time to do this because so many families get together on this Sunday. Another nice photo to take at this time is a generation photo, including all the mothers and children in your extended family. If dads want to be in the picture, that's okay too!

YOUR OWN BACKYARD PARK

Now that the weather is getting nicer, it is fun to head for the nearest park or lake on a Sunday afternoon. But why worry about going somewhere? Create your own backyard park, where you can enjoy a mini golf course anytime. Or plan a bike parade that goes just around the block, with a picnic in the backyard.

41. Mini Golf Course

You will need: golf clubs and balls, or alternatives, such as croquet mallets and balls; yogurt containers for the holes; carpet scraps for putting greens; rocks or bricks; plastic pipes, assorted wood scraps, empty boxes, and anything else you think would make the course more fun or challenging.

To begin making your mini golf course, determine how much of your yard you will be using. Let everyone in your family sketch out ideas about what shape the course should take; then choose the one that would work best in the space you have.

Dig small holes where you want them and place clean, empty yogurt containers in them. Use your other materials to build the course, planning it so that the wood pieces and other items will guide the balls as they round corners or go through tunnels.

Place the carpet scraps in the places where you want the putting greens, and use the rocks or bricks to make parallel lanes for the balls to travel through. If you have any plastic PVC pipe, use it to make corners and angles by joining the pieces. If you have large rocks or lawn furniture in your course, a piece of cardboard or wood can become a ramp for the ball to travel up, and then splash down into a puddle or tunnel on the other side. Use your natural ground and materials such as sand, water, and mud to make other obstacles for the balls to go through or around.

Remember that your course can be changed in simple ways each time that you play, making it easier or harder to suit the ages and skill level of your players. Have fun!

42. Plan a Bike Parade

You will need: a bike for everyone; crepe-paper streamers; clothespins; playing cards

Decorate your bikes for a bike parade that is colorful and noisy! Wrap crepe-paper streamers around the handlebars of each bike, tying the streamers together and letting the ends hang down. Weave other streamers in and out of the tire spokes to make pinwheels. It is fun to alternate colors to make a striped design.

Let your imaginations run wild as you decorate your bikes for the parade. If you want, clip several playing cards to the tire spokes with clothespins. When the wheels turn, the cards make a great clicking noise as you roll along!

Plan your bike parade route through your neighborhood streets or through a nearby park. Don't be surprised if other families want to follow your lead and join the parade!

43. Artists in Action Show

You will need: assorted types of paper and art materials, such as chalk and paint; collage materials and other kinds of art materials you might want to use; clothesline or fence; clothespins or tape

Plan a Sunday afternoon artists-in-action show to take place in your own yard. Arrange the art materials you have collected on a large table, or on the ground where it will be easy for the artists to find them. Let everyone try creating artwork of different kinds. Then hang the completed works on a clothesline or along a fence.

Sidewalk chalk painting can be a part of your art show too. It is easy to use chalk on the sidewalk, and the best part is that it will wash right off with the hose or in the next rain.

Be forewarned! When your friends and neighbors see what fun your family is having, they will want to join you! I have even known neighborhoods where this activity has turned into an annual event. It brings out the artist in everyone!

JUNE DAYS

*N*ow that June is here, Sunday afternoons will seem even longer. The longest day of the year is June 21; Father's Day is on a Sunday; and summer vacations are in full swing. The weather usually provides many opportunities to enjoy the outdoors, so make it a point to do just that!

It is important, as the summertime schedule hits full force, to relax and enjoy one another's company even more. Summer days and nights are good times to reflect on ways we as Christians can live life to the fullest and appreciate our blessings as members of our family at home and our family at church. Ephesians 6:1-4 reminds us of our responsibilities as parents and children:

> Children, obey your parents in the Lord, for this is right. "Honor your father and mother"—which is the first commandment with a promise—"that it may go well with you and that you may enjoy long life on the earth."
>
> Fathers, do not exasperate your children; instead, bring them up in the training and instruction of the Lord.

Use your family time this month to talk about your family life as part of the family of God.

JUST FOR FUN

Now that the weather is great and there is more free time, spend a Sunday afternoon trying on some of these fun and different ideas for size!

44. Make Tin-can Stilts

You will need: 2 48-ounce juice cans for each pair of stilts; two lengths of thin stiff rope or clothesline, each about 5 feet long, for each pair of stilts; a puncture-type can opener

This simple version of stilts is fun and easy for everyone in the family to try. Puncture each juice can on opposite sides close to the top. Carefully pour the juice into a pitcher or glasses and save it to drink when you are through. Rinse out the cans and remove the tops.

Now thread a 5-foot length of rope through the holes in each can, holding the rope ends of one can in each hand. Stand on the cans and hold the rope ends taut. Tie the loose ends of each rope together in a knot about waist high and grip the ropes, pulling them up tightly to help you walk.

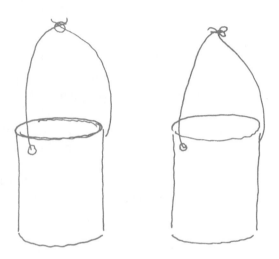

45. Make a Periscope

You will need: a narrow box with a lid, such as a shoe box; two small metal mirrors from a hardware or sporting-goods store; masking tape; scissors; glue

Set the box on end. Place one of the mirrors on the bottom of one side of the box and trace around it. Do the same on the top of the other side of the box.

Cut out the outlines to make two windows in the long box as shown; then follow the diagrams to help you place the mirrors. You might need to move the mirrors around a bit to find the best position in your particular box. When you are satisfied with their positions, glue the mirrors in place.

Try the periscope to make sure it is working. When you look through the bottom window, you should be able to see out at the top.

To finish your periscope, put the lid on the box, tape the edges, and paint it. Your new periscope can help you peek over fences, around trees, and over a windowsill down onto the yard below!

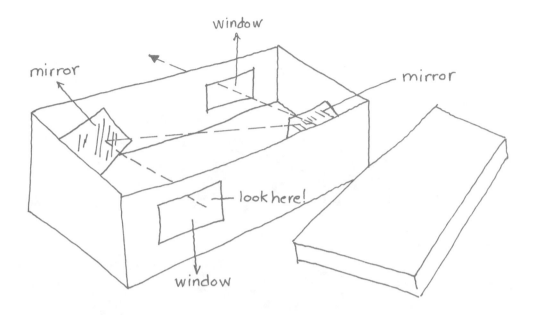

window

mirror

mirror

look here!

window

46. Make an Inner-tube Raft

You will need: a drill; a handsaw; three inner tubes, blown up; about 30 feet of rope; a board as long as three inner tubes lined up

Line up the inner tubes and lay the board across the top of them. Round the corners of the board with the handsaw—so that you won't bump against a sharp edge. Don't let more than 6 inches of the board hang over the inner tubes at the ends. You might want to sand off any rough edges on the board, and you can paint the board if you like.

Now lay the inner tubes on top of the board. Mark four drill holes on the board inside each inner tube, and two holes at each end of the board, as shown in the diagram, making sure the holes are about 1 inch from the edge of the board. Once you have drilled the holes, lay the inner tubes back on top of the board and use the rope to lace through the holes. Start from one end of the board and go over the inner tubes and in and out of the holes in the middle of the tubes, then in and out of the holes at the other end of the board and back up the other side in the same way. When you arrive back where you started, tie the ends so that the inner tubes are securely fastened to the board.

Nothing quite equals the splashing and playing that accompanies an afternoon in a local lake or swimming hole! This inner-tube raft is a project that takes a little forethought, but it is one that kids will treasure for years to come! Enjoy paddling together on this raft, or make two rafts and have a race!

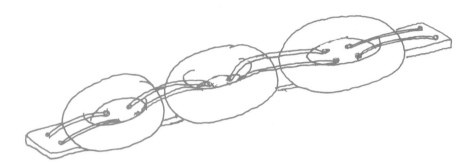

The words of Paul in Philippians remind me of the fun in the sun that water play allows all of us: "Rejoice in the Lord always!" (4:4). Summertime is certainly a time of rejoicing and a time to appreciate creation to its fullest.

HONOR YOUR FATHER

Because Father's Day always falls on a Sunday, it is a good day to have fun with your family. Preparing Dad's favorite meal is almost a given, but there are other fun things you can do as well. These mysterious games and tricks will be lots of fun for Dad, and for the rest of the family as well!

47. Invisible Messages

You will need: white paper; a water-color paintbrush; lemon juice; an iron

This old trick is still fun for all ages! Write a secret message, using lemon juice and a paintbrush. To make the message visible, press the paper with a warm iron. Presto! The message appears.

Maybe you can write Dad a special Father's Day message with this invisible ink.

48. The Mysterious Number One

You may need: pencil and paper

This is a fun and amazing trick to try. Ask everyone in your family to pick a number from 1 to 5. Don't let them tell you the number. Then tell them to double it and add 2. Now divide by 2.

Ask them to remember their original number and subtract that number from what is left. Don't tell anyone! Now, on the count of three, have everyone shout out the number they are left with. They will all shout together, "One!"

The amazing thing is that this will happen every time!

49. Tip-top Toothpicks

You will need: one box or package of toothpicks

This is a fun game to play again and again! The object of the game is to work together to build a tower made of toothpicks until it falls down.

To begin, place two toothpicks one way, then the next person places two toothpicks across the first two, going the other way, and so on. Keep count of how many toothpicks you are using, and continue to play until the tower falls over. The last person to add two toothpicks is the winner.

THOSE MIGHTY DINOSAURS

Dinosaurs are a fascinating topic for almost everyone, and especially for children. Although dinosaurs lived long, long ago, new and exciting discoveries are being made about them every day. It should be easy to find books about the lives and times of dinosaurs at your local library or bookstore. You might find a budding scientist within your family as you try some of these Sunday afternoon activities.

If you live close to a museum or science center, check the schedule to see whether they have an ongoing dinosaur exhibit, or might be sponsoring one that you can visit. Seeing life-size models of dinosaurs is an awesome experience, and one that children never will forget.

50. How Long Is a Dinosaur?

You will need: a parking lot or long sidewalk; a 25-foot tape measure; chalk

You don't need to see life-size models of dinosaurs to get an idea of how big they were compared to you and the people in your family. Find a long parking lot or a sidewalk that is fairly quiet, and take your family members along to stretch out and measure the lengths of some of the best-known dinosaurs. Use a 25-foot tape measure to start measuring, and place a person at each 10-foot mark as you move along. A piece of chalk is a great way to mark the pavement so that you can actually step back and see how long those creatures were. Here are some measurements to "try on for size":

☞ Tyrannosaurus Rex—18 feet tall, 50 feet long (its teeth were
     6 feet long!)
☞ Diplodocus—100 feet long
☞ Brontosaurus—70 feet long

51. Hatch a Dinosaur

You will need: a large balloon; newspaper; papier-mâché paste; a pin; knife or scissors; gallon milk jugs (2); cardboard scraps; heavy-duty tape; paint

Blow the balloon up as large as you can and apply torn pieces of newspaper dipped into papier-mâché paste over the balloon until it feels sturdy. Set aside for at least several days to dry. When the "egg" is dry, poke a pin through the newspaper layers to pop the balloon. Cut the egg in half in a jagged fashion and paint the inside and the outside.

Use the two milk jugs to make the baby dinosaur. Cut the bottom from one jug and slip the two jugs together to form the body. Tape the jugs together.

Trace and cut legs and stegosaurus plates from the cardboard as shown in the diagram. Use plenty of tape to fasten these pieces to the milk jugs.

Crumple up several pieces of newspaper and tape around them to mold the head shape you want. Crumple more newspaper to slip into the open spaces near the handles of the jugs, and tape all the newspaper pieces in place. Then begin layering strips of newspaper dipped into papier-mâché paste all over the dinosaur body. Cover it completely with several layers and set it aside to dry.

When the dinosaur is dry, paint it as you like, pop it into its completed egg, and see what you have hatched!

JULY DAYS

July just seems to be picnic weather, and a picnic after church on Sunday is a fun family tradition to begin. Do you and your family have a favorite picnic spot? Maybe it's on a nearby river bank, or perhaps it's just in your backyard. Wherever your family decides to picnic, make the most of hot summer weather with some of these ideas.

FAMILY PICNIC FUN

52. A Prepacked Picnic Basket

You will need: picnic basket or bag; assorted supplies (see below)

Why not make summer picnicking quick and easy by having a prepacked picnic basket, ready and waiting at all times? Keep a basket or bag in the hall closet filled with essentials: a blanket, paper plates and cups, utensils, napkins, bug repellant, a trash bag, and other things your family likes to take on picnics. Then when the mood strikes, you can easily prepare quick picnic foods such as sandwiches, juice, and fruit.

Some other nice touches to take along are a wet face cloth, a towel or two (in case there is wading water nearby), a jar with a tight lid half full of water (to fill with flowers when you arrive and set in the middle of the blanket), a book to read aloud, a checkerboard and checkers, a camera, and anything else that would be fun once you arrive at your picnic spot.

53. Flip-a-coin Picnic Spot

You will need: a penny or other coin; a packed picnic basket; blanket

After you have packed your picnic basket, start on your flip-a-coin picnic. Once you have stepped out of your door or into your car, decide together on which direction you will go, based on the flip of a coin. For example, you might want to go right, if the coin lands heads up; left, if the coin lands tails up.

From that point on, you must turn in the direction indicated by the flipped coin. Keep going, amidst the laughs and uncertainty, until you reach a spot that everyone agrees upon as a good place to have a picnic. The most important thing is not to get so far away so that you can't find your way back home again!

flip a coin

SUMMERTIME FUN

When a Sunday afternoon in July beckons to you and your family, revel in it's warmth and sunlight! Some of the ideas listed here will give you a chance to actually enjoy the heat of the day.

And if you stored snowballs in your freezer last winter, this might just be the day to take them out of the freezer and turn them into snow-cones or slushies! Just plop the snowballs into a cup or bowl and pour a splash of your favorite juice on top. Mmmmmm!

54. Tin-can Ice Cream

You will need: 1 empty 1-pound coffee can with a lid; one #10 can with a tight-fitting lid; ice-cream ingredients (see below); crushed ice; rock salt

INGREDIENTS

1 cup milk
1 cup whipping cream
½ cup sugar
½ teaspoon vanilla extract

Put all ingredients into the coffee can and seal with the lid. Place this can inside the #10 can, and pack crushed ice between the two cans. Pour about ¾ cup of rock salt evenly over the ice, and put the lid on the #10 can.

Sit on the sidewalk or floor and roll the can back and forth among the people in your family for about 10 minutes. Open the lid on the outer can and remove the inner can. Remove the lid and scrape the ice cream mixture from the sides of the can; replace the lid. Drain the water from the larger can, replace the small can, and repack with crushed ice and rock salt. Replace the lid and roll the cans back and forth for at least 5 more minutes. Check to make sure the ice cream is done; if not, repeat the process until it is.

55. Frozen Pops

You will need: paper cups; wooden sticks or plastic spoons; assorted canned fruit (such as fruit cocktail); packages of instant pudding and milk, or your favorite fruit juices

Prepare the type of ingredients you would like to have for your frozen pops and pour an evenly spaced amount into the paper cups. Be sure not to fill the cups to the top, as liquids expand as they freeze.

Slide a wooden stick or plastic spoon into the center of each cup for the handle and set the cups in the freezer. When the pops are frozen firm, peel the paper cups away and enjoy your frozen treats on a hot summer afternoon.

56. Slip-sliding Away

You will need: an old plastic tablecloth, or any piece of smooth plastic; a garden hose and water

Lay the plastic somewhere in your yard where the hose can reach it easily and spray the plastic until it is wet and slippery. Turn off the hose, or leave it at a trickle, as you take turns running and sliding across the slippery plastic.

Note: An adult should try this before any children give it a try, just to make sure there are no sharp edges on the plastic that might catch a toe or finger.

57. Garden-hose Rainbow

You will need: sunny weather; a garden hose

Did you know it is easy to make a rainbow with an ordinary garden hose? It is! Of course, the sun must be shining, just as when a real rainbow is made. But the rest is up to you.

Stand with your back to the sun, and spray a fine mist from your hose right in front of you. Do you see a rainbow in the midst? This actually works best in late afternoon or early morning, when the sun's rays are slanting low in the sky. As you watch your rainbow, try to see if you can find all the colors in it.

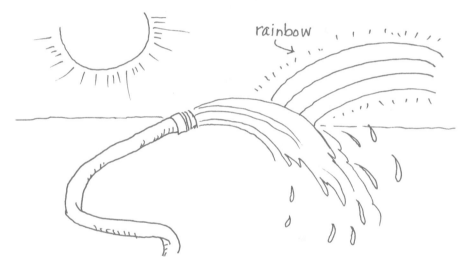

rainbow →

THE GREAT OUTDOORS

58. Backyard Campout

An outdoor camping experience is a must for a summer Sunday afternoon and evening. Actually, you may want to begin this adventure on Saturday evening and continue it through the entire weekend!

A tent isn't a necessity, but it can be nice in case there is a rain shower. A blanket, or even an old tablecloth, can serve as a temporary tent.

Teach your children a little about camping out in the great outdoors in your own backyard, before venturing farther out. Be sure to make your overnight campout as realistic as possible, taking along the things you will need in order to "rough it" as much as possible.

Be sure to take warm sleeping bags or blankets—even in the summertime, the night air can be cool. Flashlights with fresh batteries are important for everyone to have. Water canteens or clean plastic milk jugs filled with water are important for drinking, washing hands or dishes, and brushing teeth. (Yes, you still need to brush your teeth when you go camping!)

A pack of cards, or a guitar or other musical instrument are fun to bring along. And don't forget a special toy or blanket if someone has one they need to sleep with.

Be sure to take extra socks and a warm sweater or sweatshirt when you go camping. Sometimes feet get wet, and it may be chilly in the evening.

Look together at your campsite and find the most level place to place the tent. Remember that if you face your tent toward the southeast, the first rays of sunshine will wake you up right away in the morning, and you won't even need an alarm clock!

Take food with you that is easy to prepare and that everyone likes. If you have a little barbecue or a place to build a fire pit, you can cook hot dogs or chicken breasts on a stick, warm a can of beans, and end the meal with the all-time favorite camping dessert—S'mores!

To make S'mores, toast marshmallows until they are golden brown, then slide the marshmallow off the stick onto a graham cracker on which a square from a chocolate bar has been placed. Top with another graham cracker—mmmm!

It is easy to bake potatoes or corn on the cob in a fire. Just wrap them in foil and lay them in the coals to bake. Canned foods, such as stews, are good over a campfire, too. And it is easy to pop popcorn for a late-night snack!

When you remember that a camping adventure is as close as your own backyard, you have the advantage of many family afternoons and evenings to come.

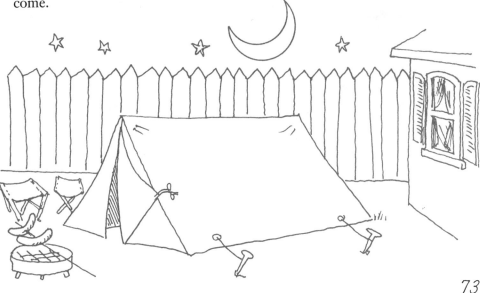

59. Campfire Games

You and your family will probably think of funny games to play as you sit around your campfire, but here are a few to get you started.

GOSSIP

With everyone sitting in a circle, have one person begin a silly message by whispering it to the person on the right. Each person in turn will whisper the message to the person on the right until the message reaches the person next to its originator. That person repeats aloud the message as he or she heard it, and the originator tells what the message really was.

SMUGGLING

With everyone sitting in a circle, one person is chosen to be "it." It stands outside the circle with eyes closed, while the people in the circle pass around a small stone or other item. Everyone moves the stone around the circle, sometimes making false passes, as if it were being passed, when it really wasn't. At any time, It may look and try to determine who really has the stone. When It thinks he or she knows who has the stone, It taps that person's hand. If right, the person caught becomes the new It; if not, the game continues until It discovers who really is holding the stone.

> Worship the LORD in the splendor of his holiness.
> (Psalm 96:9)

AUGUST DAYS

*M*y family and I are fortunate enough to live near the beach. We make frequent trips there throughout the year, and some of my best childhood memories revolve around the beach that was close to my home.

Even if you don't live near an ocean beach, some of the things to do listed here could be tried at a lake or river. And the chances are that sometime in your life, you might have the chance to visit an ocean, so reading through these ideas will put you one step closer to enjoying the beach when that day finally comes.

SAND ANTICS

60. Sandcasting

You will need: a disposable aluminum pie plate for each person; seashells, small rocks or pieces of driftwood; plaster of paris; empty milk cartons; water

By making a sandcasting at the beach, you will have something to take back with you as a memento. When you purchase the plaster of paris, be sure to read the instructions on the package before you leave for the beach. Empty milk cartons make good containers for carrying and pouring clean water in which to mix the plaster when you arrive at the beach.

Pour dampened sand into the pie plates, and press or draw a design with your fingers. Add to the design the seashells and other small items you have found on the beach. Depending upon the way you decorate your design, it could end up looking like a sun or a starfish.

When you are pleased with the design, spoon plaster of paris into the depressions you have made in the sand, then gently pour a ½-inch thick layer over the entire design.

When the plaster is completely dry, turn the plate over and tap on it gently to remove the sandcasting.

61. Sand Sculpture

You will need: assorted containers and small buckets; small sand shovels

Some beaches have world-famous sand sculpture contests! You and your family can spend a Sunday afternoon creating your own sculpture gallery at the beach by using the assorted containers and buckets you have brought with you.

Fill the containers with damp sand and pack it down; then turn the containers upside down and begin to create your sculpture. There is more to sculpting than just building a castle. How about an alligator or a dragon? A snake or a walrus? Of course, castles are still fun to build, especially when you add a moat, with real water flowing through it!

Remember to pay attention to which way the tide is going, so that your sculpture isn't ruined before you are finished with it.

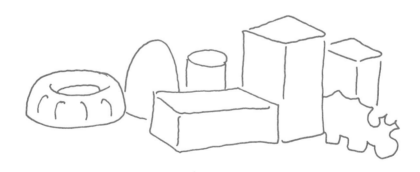

62. Rock and Shell Creations

You will need: heavy-duty glue; wiggly eyes; rocks and pebbles; assorted shells; driftwood; string; a candle; nail and hammer

To make wind chimes out of shells, or rock and pebble animals, it is best to collect the supplies from the beach and take them home to create your artistic work on another Sunday afternoon.

To make rock and pebble animals, try positioning the rocks on top of each other to create the shapes of animals. When you are happy with the animals you have made, glue the rocks together and add wiggly eyes so the animals can see!

Wind chimes are beautiful to make from shells that you have collected on your day at the beach. Decide which shells you would like to use; then carefully use a candle to warm up a nail to make a hole in the shell. Carefully tap the hammer on the nail to make the hole. (Warming the nail first will help.) If you can find shells that already have small holes in them, use these shells first.

Once you have shells with holes in them, tie a string or piece of yarn through each shell and tie it on the piece of driftwood.

Hang your completed wind chime in a place where the gentle summer breezes will blow, to remind you of your Sunday at the beach.

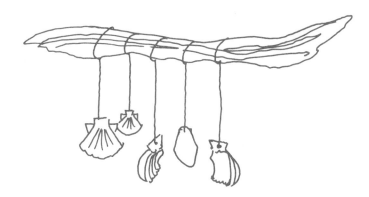

63. Tidepool Treasures

You will need: one plastic liter soda bottle for each person, or a clean, empty milk carton; clear plastic wrap; rubber bands

Tide pools, pools left by an ebbing tide, are one of the most fascinating parts of God's creation at the beach. Within a tide pool, there is an entire little world of creatures that exist together in harmony. Children and adults alike love to explore tide pools, touching the soft petals of the sea anemones to see them curl, and watching little hermit crabs scurry busily to and fro.

Making underwater scopes can help you see the creatures and events in a tide pool all the more clearly. Cut a section from the middle of the liter bottle, or cut the top and bottom from the milk carton. Tightly fasten a piece of clear plastic wrap to one end of the bottle or carton with a rubber band.

To use the scope, push the covered end into the pool and peer into it. The plastic wrap will help calm the pool and will seem to magnify everything as you look closely.

It is a great idea to take a book about tide-pool creatures with you to the beach, to help you identify the things you see.

STAR GAZING

The nights of August are such nice warm evenings that many people enjoy staying up late to watch the stars, look for constellations, and enjoy the last month before fall. Although star gazing will mean extending your Sunday afternoons into later evenings and nights, it will be well worth the change to enjoy some of nature's greatest sights.

Many books and activities to help you learn about the stars and constellations can be borrowed or bought, but one of the most fun items to look for is a package of glow-in-the-dark stickers that show the planets and stars. It is fun to put these stickers on the ceiling of a closet or bedroom and shine a flashlight on them just before bedtime, going to sleep by the light of the stars!

64. Make Your Own Planetarium

You will need: an old black umbrella (or a round oatmeal box or tin can with bottom removed); flashlights; straight pins; a book or chart that shows common constellations; scissors; tracing paper; pencils; black paper

After studying the constellations you are most likely to see and come to recognize, decide which you would like to include in your own planetarium. Some favorites you might like to include are the Big Dipper, the Little Dipper, the Northern Star, or Ursus Major and Minor.

If you are using an umbrella, trace the constellations onto a piece of tracing paper from your chart; then place the paper on the umbrella and use a straight pin to make pin holes where the stars would be. To make the stars light up, turn off the lights in the room, hold the umbrella open, and turn the flashlight into the umbrella and toward the ceiling. Can you see the constellations on the ceiling?

If you are using the oatmeal box or tin can, you can trace the constellation dots onto a circular piece of black paper. Tape the circle onto the end of the oatmeal box or can, turn the flashlight inward toward the end of the box or can, and learn to identify your constellations!

65. Meteor Watch

You will need: an astronomy chart or magazine that pinpoints your area; lawn chairs

In August, from about the 10th to the 13th, there is a spectacular show in the heavens featuring a meteor shower that lights up the sky. Many people wait all year to see this shower, one of the biggest of the year. Although the best time to really see these meteors is after midnight, you don't need to stay up that late to see them.

Gather your family and friends together for that Sunday evening, and spend a night of awe watching the stars as they seem to fall from the sky.

About 100 million meteors are thought to enter the earth's atmosphere each day, but most of them vaporize too high in the atmosphere for us to see. On some occasions, fragments of meteors have been known to fall to the ground, but this is quite rare. If this does happen, these are called meteorites.

The meteor shower that occurs during August is called the Perseid shower and can be seen in the northeast portion of the sky, near the constellation Perseus.

The heavens declare the glory of God;
the skies proclaim the work of his hands.
(Psalm 19:1)

ZOO FUN

66. A Trip to the Zoo

What summer is complete without at least one trip to the zoo? Sunday afternoon is a good time to visit the zoo and watch the animals as they laze through the hazy, lazy, days of summer.

If there is not a zoo near you, perhaps there is a wild animal park or a natural animal habitat, or even a petting zoo. Many times when people vacation in other cities, they take in the sights of the zoo as part of a whirlwind tour. If you can find even a small zoo or pet habitat close to home, you and your family will probably enjoy it more, because you can actually spend quite a bit of time watching the animals as they are fed and trained—or even as they snooze.

As with any other outing, be sure to take along snacks and wet cloths to wash hands, especially if animals are petted. Call ahead if you can, and plan your afternoon so that you will be at the zoo when some of the animals are being fed, or when there is a particular animal performance or show you can attend.

A sketchbook or camera is always nice to take along to record the interesting and funny things as they happen to you at the zoo.

Help your children to see and notice different things about the animals you are watching. Can they imitate the walk of the giraffe? How do the elephants swing their trunks? What funny sound do the penguins make as they dive into the water?

Remember that besides the gift of time, one of the greatest gifts you can give your children is the gift of being able to see things around them as created by a God who is full of life and laughter.

67. Zoo Pillows

You will need: paper; pencils; fabric paints or crayons; brushes; muslin or other plain fabric; pillow stuffing

When you return home from the zoo, have everyone in the family draw a favorite animal. Encourage them to sketch the animal first, making it as large as they can.

Then, using fabric crayons or paints, transfer the drawings to the muslin fabric, to make pillows as a remembrance of the family trip to the zoo. Sew each pillow top to a handmade or purchased pillow and enjoy them for years to come. Be sure to have the artists sign and date their work for the future!

God made the wild animals according to their kinds.
(Genesis 1:25)

SEPTEMBER DAYS

When we think of September, many of us think about new beginnings. Although the first day in January is officially the start of a new year, for many people the crisp days of September remind us of going back to school, wearing new shoes, and bringing jackets and sweaters out of the closet to prepare for the coming cool weather.

Labor Day, one of the official holidays during the month of September, is a time to relax from our work and enjoy some family fun. A discussion about Labor Day can also be an opportunity to teach your children about the joy that comes from learning how to do a job and the satisfaction that comes from completing the task.

AROUND THE HOUSE

68. Fix-it Day

You will need: a large box or other container

Every family has items that break or just need minor repairs—from a button that needs to be reattached to a book with a torn page. When you designate a "fix-it" box, and even a "fix-it" day, not only will you be sure that items will be repaired regularly, but you also will give your children the skills necessary to evaluate what can or cannot be repaired and to use tools properly. Most important, you will give your children the gift of self-confidence in their abilities.

Throughout the month, have family members who have something in need of repair put their items into the "fix-it" box; then, on the designated day, gather everyone together with the tools you will need and spend some time repairing all the items in the box. This is a great way to share time with one another, in addition to teaching your children the proper way to use tools of all kinds.

69. Three Boxes for Cleaning

You will need: three boxes; felt-tip pens

Let everyone in the family help decorate the three boxes with felt-tip pens, labeling them "TO SAVE," "TO GIVE AWAY," "TO THINK ABOUT." Then spend one or more Sunday afternoons working together to sort and clean out drawers, cupboards, and closets that have been neglected or allowed to accumulate clutter of all sorts.

Help one another determine if an item is worth saving, or if it is something that is outgrown or no longer useful for anyone in your own family. Whenever possible, find ways to reuse items, rather than just throwing them away. Fill a bag for a local charitable organization, or plan a garage or rummage sale. And there's another idea for a Sunday afternoon!

> Whatever you do, work at it with all your heart, as working for the Lord.
>
> (Colossians 3:23)

HONOR YOUR FAMILY

Some time ago, someone decided to create a special day to honor the oldest members of the family—grandparents! Although we don't really need a special day to honor these important people in our lives, sometimes making one day special is a great way to show children how to love, honor, and respect the people they love.

Many families today live miles and miles apart, while in other situations, children, parents, and grandparents live under one roof, just as they did in times past. In whatever situation your family finds itself, there are numerous ways to share the joy of a Sunday afternoon! (And if there are no grandparents in the lives of your children, why not find a couple to "adopt"—everyone will benefit!)

70. A Special Meal

You will need: table settings for everyone; a favorite meal; candles; flowers or other decorations for the table; place cards; felt-tip pens; slides or photos for the "talent"

All of us appreciate being invited to a meal where we are the honored guests! Invite the grandparents or other older members or friends of your family for a Sunday afternoon meal that everyone will enjoy.

By planning far enough ahead, you and your family can design a talent show that features the honored guests and their lives. Use a title such as "This Is Your Life," and locate slides, photos, or other memorabilia that will be fun to share with everyone at the meal. Be sure to practice any acting that may be required if you choose to act out the highlights of the guests' lives, rather than read or show slides or photos.

Does your family share an ethnic heritage? Perhaps your meal can consist of foods that reflect that heritage. Or perhaps your family has traveled together to a country that features a food that you seldom take time to prepare, but that would be enjoyed by your guests.

As you prepare the meal, have other family members help with the preparations—cleaning vegetables, setting the table, making place cards.

If you like, arrange to provide "limousine" service to the honored guests, making sure to pick them up in plenty of time for the meal.

The entertainment should be presented at the end of the meal. If you choose not to have entertainment, be sure to thank the grandparents or other guests for all they do in your lives.

71. Round-robin Video or Tape

You will need: a video recorder and blank videotapes (or cassette recorder and blank cassette tapes); any props you think might add to the video

Because families are scattered so far and wide these days, make a video card or audiotape to record messages, songs, and other thoughts. You might make it a point to do this at least one Sunday afternoon a month, or you might want to add to a tape every few weeks, as things occur in your lives.

What fun for a distant grandparent or other family member to regularly receive a tape that shows or tells about a baby's growth, a child's first lost tooth, or a first performance on the trumpet!

In times past, when paper and time were scarce, people would often share a single letter with many other people in their lives. When one person or family finished reading the letter, they would often add a note to it before sending it on to the next person. This saved rewriting news that already had been written. As this letter went around, it became known as a round-robin letter. When it returned to the originator, a new letter was started.

In the same way a round-robin letter was used, a round-robin tape could be started and added to from one household to another. Family and friends from near and far would enjoy being a part of this!

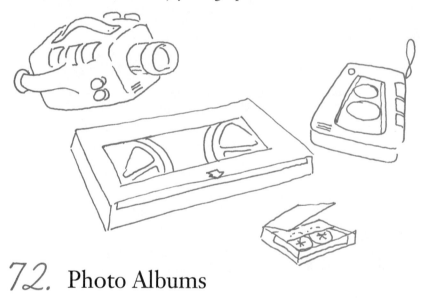

72. Photo Albums

You will need: old family albums and photos; time

Make plans to spend a long Sunday afternoon looking through old family photos and photo albums with your family. There is a feeling beyond words when people can see their connection with the generation that came before them.

Point out photos of special times and places in your lives and in the lives of your ancestors. Be sure to add the stories that have been passed down to you, giving your children a sense of their place in the chain of love you call family.

Be sure to include photos of your children, too, and tell them the stories that make them a special part of the same family. Children never tire of hearing stories about how their mother and father met, when they were born, and where they lived when they were only two years old.

> Gray hair is a crown of splendor;
> it is attained by a righteous life.
> (Proverbs 16:31)

FALL DAYS

There is a crispness to the air in the fall that everyone enjoys. From the smallest child to the oldest adult, nothing quite matches the feeling that comes from scuffling through fallen leaves, the smell of a fireplace on the first cool night of the year, and the crunchy bite of a freshly picked apple.

Celebrate the season on a Sunday afternoon by getting out in the cool air and enjoying the world that God created!

73. Plant a Tree

You will need: a place to dig in the ground (or a half-barrel full of soil); a shovel; a bucket of water; a small tree of your choice

A family tree can hold a place of honor in your own family's life—the family tree, that is, that will grace your yard for many years to come. Use your Sunday afternoon to visit a nursery or tree farm in your area to choose the perfect tree to plant in your yard.

A tree that changes with the seasons, perhaps a flowering tree of some sort, will offer the most changes for your family to watch and observe. At different times throughout the year, the tree will be bare, then have buds, leaves, and flowers. A fruit tree will offer the same variety, with the addition of edible gifts of fruits. An evergreen tree is just that—always green, never totally losing its leaves during the year. Evergreen trees are reminders of God's love for us—never changing, always green and growing.

Whichever tree your family chooses, check with a nursery worker about how deep to dig the hole, whether the tree needs special care, and the best time for planting. Then on your designated day, gather together to dig the hole and plant and water the tree.

If you live in an apartment, or for other reasons have no available ground, place the half-barrel of soil in a large planter and plant your tree in that. Also, consider a tree that grows well indoors—such as a ficus.

As you finish, you might choose this time to thank God for all trees and growing things, and especially for your own family time.

74. Rake and Run

You will need: a sunny day; rakes; fallen leaves; camera and film

Fallen leaves, one of the sure signs that winter is coming, can be both fun and frustrating! Spend a Sunday afternoon having fun while making short work of the frustration.

If you have no leaves in your yard, or insufficient leaves for this activity, check with some of the neighbors in your area to see if you can rake their leaves for them. As you rake the leaves into big piles, try different things. Who can make the biggest pile? Who can find the smallest leaf? The biggest?

Who can find the leaf that is the reddest? The yellowest? The one that has the most colors?

The real fun comes when all the leaves are raked into the biggest pile you can make—time to run! Take turns with your children running and jumping into the leaves, being sure to take pictures of everyone as they are buried. Of course, part of this fun involves reraking all the leaves back into a pile when you are done. This is a guaranteed memory-maker and one that will always be requested when the leaves begin to fall from year to year.

75. A Tree-house Getaway

You will need: a tree with a sturdy base and center; scraps of lumber; hammers; nails; other assorted materials and tools

We all need a place all our own to escape to when the day has been long. How about building a place for your family to go whenever the mood strikes?

Choose a suitable tree in your yard. Measure and cut the lumber scraps to build the base of the house. Will you need steps, or a ladder to reach the tree house? If so, you can build or purchase one just for this purpose.

Make your house simple but safe. (You might want to check out a library book on simple carpentry, if you haven't done much of this kind of work before.)

Decide together whether your house will have solid sides or just a railing. Will it have a roof, or will the tree branches and leaves serve as the roof? As you work together to build your own getaway, talk and discuss the different things you want to do in your completed tree house—have a "tree warming," host a tea party, plan a sleep-over. Create and plant the thoughts of this safe place to go, to talk, giggle, and share hopes and dreams as a family throughout the years to come!

[God] has made everything beautiful in its time.
(Ecclesiastes 3:11)

OCTOBER DAYS

O ctober—a month of falling leaves and settling into a cozy routine. October usually finds those in cooler climates choosing indoor activities when the weekend rolls around. But if you live in a cooler climate, why limit yourself? Sundays in October are often the crisp kind that put rosy cheeks on everyone! And even in a warm climate, October is a good month for families to enjoy God's gifts of creation in special ways. Browse through the ideas here for a special way to spend October Sunday afternoons with your family.

DISCOVERY WALKS

On one of those lazy Sunday afternoons when it seems to be time to get out of the house, make a "discovery walk" your excursion for the day. Sunday afternoon walks and drives have long been a part of family life—times to spend together while enjoying new surroundings, to delight in the day of rest that God created. And these excursions are not usually very costly, although people will tell you their worth is invaluable! Sometimes exploring the world around you can make coming home seem even more fun.

In the hustle and bustle of everyday family life, it can be easy not to notice the small wonders in the world around you—an inchworm creeping up the stem of a twig, a small garden snake sunning itself on a rock, the crunch of autumn leaves as feet scuffle through them—all these are awesome reminders of God's creations. In the first chapter of Genesis, we read about the creation of the world and all that is in it. "And God saw that it was good." Have you?

76. Circle Around

You will need: a piece of rope or string, or a hula hoop; magnifying glass; pad of paper; pencil; crayons or felt-tip pens

Come out of the house on a nice fall afternoon, and the children can run circles around adults as they begin to explore and discover the world around them! Place a boundary around their circle as you begin the discovery process together.

Choose a spot and place the string or hoop on the ground to make a circle. Get down on the ground together and begin to notice and point out the variety of things you see within the circle. What is the ground like within the circle? Grassy! Sandy? Is it full of pebbles? Are there any bugs or worms? How about ants? Look closely. What are the bugs doing?

Begin to draw and write your circle observations on the pad of paper, perhaps with one family member recording everyone's ideas. Set a time limit on your discovery recording; then, if you have time, choose another spot to explore and compare. What things are the same? What things are different in your new circle?

77. Follow the Year

You will need: camera and film (or paper); felt-tip pens; crayons; paper; tape measure

When you and your family are out walking, pick out a unique or unusual tree in your yard or neighborhood. Use this tree as the focus of a year-long project. Take photographs of the tree in each season, or draw the tree as a poster to reflect the changes your family observes. Besides the changes in the tree's appearance, what other changes do you notice? Do different birds or animals live in or near the tree during different seasons?

You might also want to take a rubbing of the bark of the tree. To make a bark rubbing, lay a piece of paper over the bark and gently rub a crayon back and forth. Watch the pattern of the bark emerge!

Or measure the tree's diameter and height, then keep track of it's growth on a chart. One fun way to keep track of a tree's growth and a child's growth is to make side-by-side charts in a doorway or on a refrigerator.

78. Compass Walk

You will need: compass; map; felt-tip pen; camera and film (optional)

Do you sometimes feel as if you live by going around in circles? Or maybe you live in the city and find yourself going in squares or rectangles, from block to block. It's a proven fact that when people are lost, they do walk around in circles as they try to find their way home.

Not many people today find the need to use a compass in their daily work, but the skills needed to use a compass are invaluable. Beginning with the basics of knowing directions—north, south, east, and west—and the other skills needed in reading a map and using a compass, you and your family can have a fun Sunday afternoon walk that also is educational!

Familiarize yourselves with the compass, and practice using it in your house and then in your yard. Talk about the directions and note the direction of east and west, in accordance with the rising and setting of the sun. This is a very real experience to which children can relate, although, depending on their ages, they may never actually have seen a sunrise or sunset! Perhaps this Sunday will be the day you all arise early enough to enjoy the first rays sent forth by the sun!

Let the compass guide you and your family on a walk through your neighborhood or a nearby park. Use the compass to keep you in a straight line. Traipsing through unbroken paths can lead to some interesting discoveries. But what if your straight line leads you right into a rock, or a grove of prickly bushes, or even a creek? In that case, try to go around, across, or carefully through your discovery.

With your felt-tip pen, mark on the map the path you take. Be sure to take a photograph of anything interesting you find along your way!

> God saw all that he had made, and it was very good.
> **(Genesis 1:31)**

ART SMART

The world around us is full of light and color. Children, especially, seem to perk up when they are exposed to that beauty. As a parent and teacher, I find children stimulated and excited about color. There are many more choices in colors than I ever knew as a child. If you don't think this is so, take a look at a box of crayons—especially a box of 96 crayons! Even the names of the colors today reflect a bright and varied world.

As a teacher, I also find that even the youngest children know their colors before they begin preschool. Because this is so, I make a point of adding to their knowledge of color and art by exposing them to some of the famous paintings of the art masters. Simple terms and familiarity with art styles is a wonderful gift to give a child. Try making art the focus of one of your Sunday afternoons for an especially exciting time!

79. Visit an Art Gallery or Museum

You will need: a museum or art gallery to visit; a sketch pad and pencil for each person

There is no right or wrong way to visit a museum or art gallery! Everyone will be drawn to or fascinated by different types of artwork and displays. Children are no exception, but there are some helpful suggestions for visiting museums or galleries so that everyone gets the best out of it.

Take along a sketch pad and pencil for each family member. This is a great way to keep everyone's interest as you journey through the art treasures. Encourage everyone to sketch a favorite painting or statue as you are walking through the exhibits. Perhaps they will only want to sketch part of the painting, or a statue may inspire them to make a sketch to duplicate later in play-dough or clay. If nothing else, the sketch pad will serve as a doodle pad if boredom sets in.

Here are some other helpful hints to keep in mind:

✓ Pace yourself. It would be difficult to take in everything in an art gallery or museum, even a small one. Most people tend to walk toward the right when they enter a display area. Find which simple directional focus works best for your family, and then continue in that pattern. Children always do best when there is consistency they can depend on.

✓ Begin at the beginning. Many galleries and museums are set up with a logical progression from room to room, but don't be limited to this. When you are beginning to enjoy art, sequence and pace are unimportant.

✓ Have a child's eye. You can help your children appreciate artwork by trying to see it from their viewpoint. Perhaps a large painting seems overwhelming to them—what small part of that can you focus on? How about the expression of the child in the garden? Some displays will be especially appealing to children, such as a display of toys or armor. Many museums also have outdoor sculpture gardens, which make a nice break from inside air.

✓ Don't forget the building itself. Many buildings that house artwork are fascinating. Be sure to point out pillars, molded figureheads, and other things of artistic interest.

80. Meet the Artists

You will need: samples of artists' work (sometimes postcards from museums will feature their work); books about artists; paper; pencils; crayons and felt-tip pens; a mirror; an assortment of hats or other props

Whenever possible, look with your children at different types and styles of art. Children's picture books often have beautiful artwork that lends itself to an examination of its style and method, such as crayon, collage, or fingertip painting. Help your children notice the differences and similarities in art styles, and try to duplicate them yourselves.

Matisse, for example, used a style of paper cutouts when he was ill. These cutouts resemble a type of artwork I call positive/negative designs. When a shape is cut out of a folded piece of paper (without destroying the border), you can see both a negative and a positive design. Try this with your family, and see what you can create!

It is also fun to try to create a Picasso-type portrait. After everyone looks at several examples of Picasso's work, place a sheet of paper and a pencil for each person on a table. Have everyone place the point of the pencil in the center of the paper. Then, have them close their eyes and talk them through the creation of a portrait.

You might say, "All right, first draw an oval for the face. Then add a nose. Now a mouth. How about the eyes? Ears?" Continue through the entire face, and then let everyone take a look at their "Picasso-type" drawing.

Most artists, at some point in their lives, draw or paint a self-portrait. Help your children understand the difference between a portrait (a drawing of another person) and a self-portrait (a drawing of oneself).

Position a mirror at the children's level and let everyone choose a hat or other prop to include in their portrait. Then have them look in the mirror and draw themselves on the paper. (When trying this with young children, it is sometimes helpful to draw the facial oval before they begin, to ensure that they take advantage of the full sheet of paper!) Let everyone in the family add color to their paintings and hang them up in your home where everyone can see them!

FAMILY BREAKFAST BEGINNINGS

You've heard it said that a family should eat at least one meal together a day. Well, it's true! And breakfast is a good meal to eat together.

The beginning of a fresh new day is also a wonderful time to have family devotions. For one week, make it a point to plan a breakfast devotion around the words in Ecclesiastes 3:1-11, a great passage to memorize together, beginning with the words, "There is a time for everything, and a season for every activity under heaven."

81. Breakfast Brunch

You will need: special brunch recipes and necessary ingredients; any decorations you desire; hearty appetites

Kick off your week of breakfast devotions on Sunday with a breakfast brunch. Mmmm! Is there anything as good as a delicious meal prepared together and enjoyed by all? Perhaps what is so fun about brunches is that the foods are not often our everyday fare. A brunch is a good time to try new recipes that may take a little longer than usual to prepare.

Maybe the fun of brunches is simply that they are the bridge between two meals—breakfast and lunch—so they can be eaten at a more leisurely pace. Or maybe brunches are so enjoyable because they usually occur on a Saturday or Sunday, times when families look forward to a change from the weekday routine.

Whatever the reason, a Sunday brunch is a great way to spend time together on a Sunday after church! Whenever possible, choose recipes that can be at least partially prepared ahead of time, and use this time to try new and different taste treats. Of course, it is always a good idea to include a few family favorites as well!

Think about your brunch before you begin. Do you want to work out a theme, such as a Mexican meal? Will you invite another family, or other guests? Will you eat outside in a picnic, or try a buffet? Decide some of these details and make notes about what you want to do, so that every family member will have a say in your choices and a job to do when it's time to get to work!

Here are just a few simple recipes to think about to help you get started.

FRUIT KABOBS

You will need: your favorite fruits; knife; bamboo skewers or long toothpicks; lemon juice; flavored yogurt

Clean and cut your favorite fruits into small pieces. Fasten the pieces onto the skewers or toothpicks, alternating as you go. To prevent apples from turning brown, dip them in lemon juice.

When you are pleased with the kabobs, cover them with plastic wrap and refrigerate until you are ready to eat. They can be dipped in your favorite flavor of yogurt, if you like.

BREAKFAST SUNDAE

You will need: your favorite flavor of yogurt; several kinds of fresh or canned fruit; crunchy cereal or granola; raisins, coconut, chopped nuts; sundae bowls; spoons

Place several spoonfuls of yogurt into each sundae bowl. Layer on one kind of fruit, then more yogurt. Repeat with other fruit several times. When your sundae is high enough, sprinkle on crunchy cereal or granola, raisins, coconut, and chopped nuts. Yummy!

FANCY PANCAKES

You will need: your favorite pancake batter; grill or frying pan; spatula and other cooking utensils; syrups, applesauce, whipped cream, fruits, other favorite toppings

Although you may have pancakes on a regular basis, during brunch there is more time to eat them. They are so quick to cook, and there are so many different ways to top them that everyone can be creative on his or her own plate.

Place all the pancake toppings your family likes in bowls or containers and make a stack of your favorite cakes. Then let family members finish their own pancake feast with whipped cream, fruits, syrups, chopped nuts, and anything else that strikes their fancy.

In another variation, fillings can be rolled up inside the pancakes. Or fun pancake shapes and letters of the alphabet can be made by dribbling the pancake batter from a spoon or from a squeeze bottle. You can even write the names of the people in your family in pancake batter!

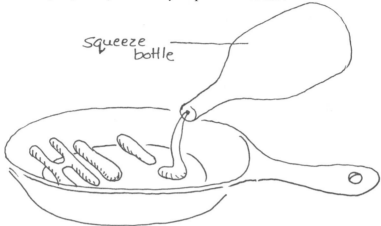

squeeze bottle

APPLE HARVEST

No matter which part of the country you live in, harvest time in the fall is highlighted by the beautiful colors and the crisp-crunchy sound of biting into a freshly picked apple. Apples seem to be one of everyone's favorite fruit treats, either eaten just as they are or cooked into apple cake, apple butter, apple crisp, or applesauce.

82. Apple-picking Afternoon

You will need: an apple tree or apple orchard; bushel baskets or boxes; a ladder

If you don't live where you can actually go and pick your own apples, don't give up! There are many open markets or farmers' markets, even in cities, which carry a large variety of freshly picked apples during harvest time.

If you can go to an orchard, or even to your own tree, learn to look for apples that are ripe and ready for picking. Depending upon the color of the apples, you will need to be sure that they are ripe before you begin picking. Also check the ground around the trees for any apples that may have fallen and be only slightly bruised—these are great for applesauce!

When you have picked your apples, take them home and store them in a cool place. If you have access to a cider press, it is great fun to press your own apples for cider. Besides eating your apples uncooked, be sure to try some new recipes for apple cake, pie, or bread. Here is an easy recipe for applesauce.

MICROWAVE APPLESAUCE

You will need: 6 apples; paring knife; ½ cup water; microwave-proof bowl with lid; microwave oven; sugar and cinnamon to taste

Peel and core about 6 apples; then cut the apples into fairly large chunks and place them in a microwave-proof bowl with a lid. Put about ½ cup of water in the bowl. You might want to wait until the applesauce is cooked to add sugar and cinnamon, because some apples are naturally sweet tasting.

Cover the apples and cook on high for 2 minutes; then stir. Cook for another 2 minutes, stir, and check for softness. When the apples are soft enough to stir into sauce, you have cooked them enough. Taste and add seasonings now if you like. Mmmmmm!

83. Apple-seed Fun

You will need: at least one large and one small apple; a knife; acrylic or tempera paint; paper or cloth

It is fun to guess how many seeds are in an apple. You would think that the largest apple would have the most seeds, but this is not usually the case.

Have everyone guess the number of seeds and write the guess on a slip of paper. Cut one of the apples open and count the seeds. Then cut the second apple open and count its seeds. Compare the two—which apple had the most seeds?

It is fun to cut an apple open first in the conventional way (from stem to bottom), and then in the "star" way—from side to side across the middle. When you do this, point out the star shape that the apple and seeds make.

Apples cut in these different ways are fun to make apple prints with, too. Press the cut apples into acrylic or tempera paint and then onto a sheet of paper or cloth.

NOVEMBER DAYS

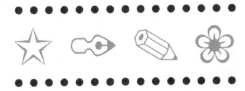

November is often thought of as a month for thankfulness—not only because the Thanksgiving holiday falls in November (for U.S. citizens), but also because we know that we are nearing the beginning of Advent, when we prepare to celebrate the gift of God's Son, Jesus. Enjoy these Sunday afternoon family-time suggestions, remembering throughout the month to give praise and thanks for all of God's gifts!

FOR THE BIRDS

Whether you live in the city or in the country, you have a backyard jungle at your fingertips! There is something rewarding and relaxing about stepping outside in any kind of weather and being able to notice the small birds and animals around you.

Oh, you don't think there are many small birds or animals in your city lot? Well, not only will a Sunday afternoon spent checking out your yard show you the wildlife living there, but trying some of these ideas might invite more of God's creatures to visit your own jungle.

84. Open for Business

You will need: a good location; bird seed; the feeder of your choice (see the following for the items needed to make your own feeder)

Both late fall and early winter are good times to begin feeding birds, but only if you are sure that you will continue to feed them throughout the winter. Once you begin to put food out for birds, they will really begin to depend upon you!

There are many books about birds, and books about bird feeders that you can make or buy. Following are a few simple ideas, along with a list of what some of the more common kinds of birds like to eat. Sometimes birds change their minds, though!

Before you begin, think about where you will put the feeder. Is it in a place that you can see and enjoy watching the birds? Will it be easy to fill with feed and to clean? Will it be safe from neighborhood cats or racoons?

Once you have thought through all these things, try your hand at making a bird feeder some Sunday afternoon. Most of the feeders suggested here are easy enough to finish in an afternoon, or you can purchase one to get you started on this great family hobby.

FEEDING PLATFORM

A stake or post driven into the ground can form the base for a feeding platform. Nail a square or rectangular piece of plywood on the top of the post; then nail strips of wood to the sides of the plywood to prevent the seed from blowing off.

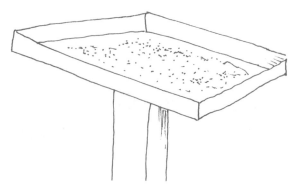

MILK CARTON OR JUG FEEDER

A clean, dry milk carton or plastic gallon jug will make a good feeder if you cut the sides out as shown, weight the bottom with a rock, and push a piece of dowel or stick through the bottom for the birds to sit on. To hang the feeder from a tree branch, tie a length of cord to the handle of the jug, or through a hole punched in the top of the carton.

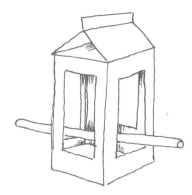

A BUFFET TREE

You can hang a variety of bird treats from a single tree to try to attract an assortment of birds. Stale pieces of bread cut with cookie cutters make good food for birds, especially if spread lightly with peanut butter and rolled in bird seed. Peanuts, carrot pieces, popcorn, and cranberries can be strung together like a necklace and hung from a tree branch. Fat and grease from cooking can be melted and poured into a paper cup; when the grease hardens, the paper can be peeled away and the fat can be hung from a tree branch.

Check with other bird experts in your area and see what other kinds of bird treats you might want to try in your own backyard.

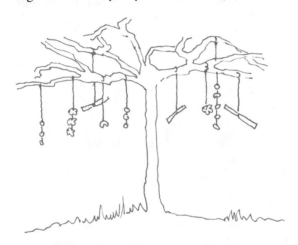

FAVORITE FOODS OF COMMON BIRDS

- ➤ Sparrow, Junco, Finch—sunflower seeds, nuts, and corn
- ➤ Blackbird, Cardinal, Towhee, Jay—bread crumbs, small seeds
- ➤ Nuthatch, Titmouse, Chickadee—sunflower seeds, fat, bread, cracker crumbs, peanuts
- ➤ Robin, Mockingbird, Catbird, Thrush—orange and apple bits, bread, crackers, raisins

85. Look at That Bird!

You will need: birds to watch; bird identification book; binoculars (optional)

Bird watching is an age-old family activity and one that makes every Sunday afternoon enjoyable, wherever you might be at the time. Watching birds is fun to do, whether you know anything about the birds you are watching or not. Everyone loves to watch hummingbirds as they hover around a beautiful flower or bird feeder in the garden!

I know one family that wanted bird watching to become a lifelong habit for their children, so they taught them when and what to watch for when the seasons changed. They kept a chart of the different kinds of birds that visited their yard, and the first person to spot the first bird of a different species—such as the first robin of spring—was given a reward. This was a definite motivator, and the children learned to watch carefully for birds throughout the year!

If you and your family really want to get to know the birds that inhabit your backyard or geographic area, be sure to take advantage of special catalogs, stores, and books that offer wisdom to novice and experienced bird watchers alike! A bird identification book is something every bird watcher should have. Although not a requirement, binoculars can help you identify birds from a distance. Here are some general things to keep in mind when you are beginning to identify birds:

- Is the bird bigger or smaller than a crow?
- Is the bird's head round, or crested?
- What shape is the bird's tail?
- Is the bird's bill long and pointed, or short and wide?
- What color is the bird's throat and breast?
- Does the bird flash a different color underneath its body when flying?

> Look at the birds of the air; they do not sow or reap or store away in barns, and yet your heavenly Father feeds them. Are you not much more valuable than they?
>
> (Matthew 6:26)

REMEMBRANCE DAY

In the United States and England, the month of November holds a day that is set aside just for remembering people who have been in the armed forces. On this day, people attend parades and memorial services that honor those who have served their countries.

Also in November, people in many churches celebrate All Saints Day, a day that is set aside to remember all the people who have gone before us in the church.

Why not make the idea of a remembrance day one of special importance to your family, but in a different way? Why not make one Sunday afternoon in November a time to relish your joy because you belong to the same family? Some of the ideas here are sure to appeal to you and others in your family; in addition to helping everyone remember that they have their place within your family, they are great builders of unity.

86. A Family Hug

You will need: your family

This is the easiest of all family activities, and one that very easily becomes a good habit! Hugging is an important part of everyone's life—days go better with hugs! Although there are many kinds of hugs, and even books written on the subject, it is easy to create your own family hug for daily use.

A circle hug can be one where all the family members huddle together in a circle, arms across shoulders or around waists to get as close as possible.

A sandwich hug is especially fun when the children are small—with two parents or grandparents on the outside, the kids in the middle of the sandwich, and everyone hugging everyone!

87. Family Meetings

You will need: time; your family

Meetings are popular with many families, not only when there are major decisions to be made, but also on a regular basis, as time set aside in the midst of a busy week. Some families like to follow a certain agenda, with a different person "chairing" the meeting each time. Other families like to have a more informal meeting, where everyone has fun talking, eating (!), then perhaps end the meeting with a fun event such as a board game or card game.

Making a habit of Sunday afternoon family meetings is a habit that can carry over many years into the future, even when you are a grandparent!

88. Make a Family Flag

You will need: paper; felt-tip pens; large pieces of fabric such as felt or burlap; scissors; assorted felt pieces; fabric glue, or needle and thread

Throughout the years, many families have handed down a family crest, emblem, or other significant mark to the generations that followed them. This is true for many families in Scotland and Ireland, for example. With the mobility of the world today, a family symbol of unity can be a thing of pride for all family members, and one that is fun to create.

Talk together with the members of your family about what things make your family unique or special. Do you ski? Raise guinea pigs for show? Are you avid bowlers? Make a list of the things that everyone feels will best identify your family. Then decide upon a design that incorporates words, symbols, or drawings that reflect those things in your family. Sketch your ideas on sheets of paper; then, when everyone agrees, make pattern pieces and cut the symbols and words from felt.

Cut a large piece of fabric to make your flag. If you will be hanging the flag or displaying it from a pole, make a casing about 2 inches wide to slip a pole into and attach it to the flag.

Glue or sew the symbols and words onto the flag and display it in a window, on your front door, or on a flag pole in your yard.

BREAKING BREAD AND GIVING THANKS

Throughout the Bible, there are references to times of thanksgiving. Thanksgiving, as we know it, has been with God's people through the ages. Although we should remember to make each day a time of thanksgiving, it sometimes helps to set aside one day to focus on thanking God for the blessings and gifts in our lives.

Breaking bread together on a Sunday afternoon is a wonderful opportunity to think about the blessings and gifts in your own family's lives!

89. Visit a Bakery

You will need: bakeries in your local area to visit

Bread speaks a universal language. The book *Bread, Bread, Bread*, written by Ann Morris, with photographs by Ken Heyman, can be an eye-opener when it comes to the varieties of bread found in countries around the world.

Does your ethnic background have a special bread that is unique to it? Tortillas, baguettes, pita, bagels, chappatties, pretzels—all these are breads from a cultural tradition.

If possible, take your family to a bakery that offers a variety of breads for purchase, and choose several to take home for a bread and cheese meal. Some bakeries also offer tours of their facilities, but probably only on weekdays.

90. Make Your Own Bread

You will need: recipe ingredients; baking utensils; bread pans or a bread machine

Search through the cookbooks you have, or look in the library for books with new and different recipes to try. A simple idea is offered here, but once you begin this bread-discovery journey, your family may want to sample a bigger variety.

THE SIMPLEST BREAD

The simplest bread to make, and one that has that home-baked taste and smell, can be found in your grocery's freezer section! You will find there a variety of types of bread, and you can bake them in their original shape, or you can cut, twist, and form the loaves into pretzels, braids, and other shapes. Just follow the baking directions on the label.

91. Make Your Own Butter

You will need: clean 35-mm film canisters or small jars; heavy cream

It is fun to see how butter is made! For each person to be served, pour 1 to 2 tablespoons of cream into a film canister. Snap the lid on tightly and shake for 3 to 5 minutes (depending on how hard and fast you shake the container). When the sloshing sound becomes more of a solid thump, open the lid. You should have a round ball of soft butter, not as yellow as the butter you buy at the grocery, and not salted. Pour off any liquid, and spread your freshly made butter on your fresh bread.

> Praise the LORD.
>   Give thanks to the LORD, for he is good;
>   his love endures forever.
>
> (Psalm 106:1)

DECEMBER DAYS

*D*ecember seems to be the month when families want to spend a lot of time together, whether they do this regularly or not. The anticipation and preparation that surrounds the celebration of the birth of the Christ Chid gives families many afternoons and evenings to have fun together.

During December, families seem to observe the most traditions and recall the most treasured memories. There are parties and get-togethers with family and friends, all in the spirit of goodwill and joy. Let the suggestions here serve only as the springboard for the family events and excursions you plan to enjoy.

CHRISTMAS-TREE MEMORIES

Although purists will agree that decorating for Christmas should be done only close to December 25th, society seems to feel differently. As long as your focus remains on the true meaning of Christmas, plan a special day to focus on the tree and all its trimmings.

In my family, we keep a large wall calendar on our refrigerator during the month of December. Here we list all the important family events, parties, and "things to do" that are planned for the month. One of the highlights is the trip to choose a Christmas tree.

Whenever possible, we have tried to find a place where we could actually tramp around in the woods and cut our own tree. This hasn't always been easy, and sometimes has meant driving quite a distance! But these are the times our family remembers best.

One of those trips resulted in a new family tradition, when the large fir tree we chose came complete with a bird's nest hidden high up near the top branches. Since then, we have carefully wrapped the nest each year and then placed it on the highest branches of our Christmas tree the next year. There is an old saying that tells of the special joy that comes to a family with a bird's nest in the Christmas tree!

92. With Heart in Hand

You will need: assorted fabrics and a piece of red fabric; fusible interfacing; an iron; paper and pencil; scissors; yarn or string; felt-tip pen

A traditional Christmas greeting in years past was the design of a heart on a handprint, as if the hand is holding a heart. Some people like to think that this stemmed from the Shaker thought, or motto, "Hands to work, hearts to God." You could use this design for family Christmas ornaments this year.

Trace around each family member's hand on a piece of paper, then cut out the hands as a pattern for the fabric and interfacing. Fuse the fabric to the interfacing as instructed on the package.

Now cut small hearts from the red fabric and use a small piece of interfacing to attach a heart to the center of each handprint. Use a felt-tip pen to write each person's name and date on the handprint.

Attach a loop of fabric or string for hanging from the tree.

93. Foil Fans

You will need: double-sided foil paper, or two colors of foil paper; string or metallic thread; scissors; stapler

Cut a 2¼- by 10-inch strip of foil for each fan. If you are using two colors back to back, cut two strips for each fan.

Accordion-pleat each fan every ¼ inch; if you are using two colors, use them back to back, pleating as one piece.

When you have completed the folds, hold the pieces together and punch a hole about ¼ inch from one end. Staple the pleats together next to the hole and open the fan. Attach a length of metallic thread or string through the loop and tie for hanging.

To make a garland of fans, thread several fans onto the metallic cord, knotting the cord on either side of each fan so that it doesn't slip through.

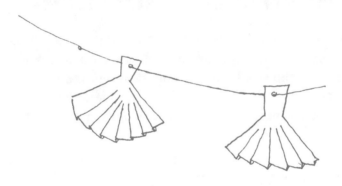

94. Angel Ornaments

You will need: white or gold paper lace doilies; scissors; glue or tape

Angels were the bearers of the good news on the night of Jesus' birth—and what more fitting ornament to make for the Christmas tree on a Sunday afternoon?

Use a lace doily as the base for the angel, rolling it into a cone shape. Cut wings from another doilie and attach to the pointed end of the cone with glue or tape. Cut a head shape from the lace scraps and attach it to the top of the cone.

This angel can be set in the branches of the tree, rather than being hung.

finished

CHRISTMAS TRADITIONS

Within every family, some Christmas holiday traditions have been carried on throughout generations, and some new ones are created each year. Some traditions last only while children are small, while others may never be dropped from the yearly calendar. Read through some of the traditions suggested here, choose one or more you would like to try, and have a fun Sunday afternoon of preparation and joy!

95. Reading the Christmas Story

You will need: a Bible or Bible storybook

One tradition in many families is to read and reread the traditional Christmas story. For some families, this means beginning with the simplest versions in children's storybooks; for others, it means reading the story as it is found in Luke.

Whether you choose to read a simplified version or the story in its entirety, the tradition of reading it each year will be one to which your children will hold throughout their lives.

Of course, it can be a lot of fun to interpret and vary the reading as your family grows and changes. In one family, the youngest children dressed up and acted out the story while one of the parents read. This was especially memorable, since they recorded it on video for future viewings!

96. A Christmas Memory Book

You will need: notebook; paper; felt-tip pens; tape or glue; family memories and keepsakes

Purchase or make a notebook that can be used for keeping a record of all your Christmas memories. Leave spaces to add photos of your holiday gatherings and special events, and include favorite thoughts from each family member. You might also want to include a gift list, or a list or envelope of special cards and letters received from friends and relatives. Children's drawings, of course, will make this book one that is treasured for years to come.

97. A Candle in the Window

You will need: electric or battery-operated candle; a window

In many cultures and traditions, it is customary to leave a candle burning in the window from Christmas Eve until Christmas morning. As a safety precaution, use an electric or battery operated candle. Turn it on at midnight on Christmas Eve and let it shine brightly until you wake up on Christmas morning. Like the star that was a guide toward the Christ Child, this candle can be a reminder to your friends and neighbors of Christ's love, shining for all people throughout all time.

98. Cookie Gift Tags

You will need: refrigerated cookie dough; rolling pin; cookie cutters or knife; drinking straw; frosting; plastic wrap; ribbon

Spend the afternoon making delectable cookie gift tags. Make your own sugar-cookie dough that can be rolled out, or purchase a roll from your grocery store. Roll the dough to ¼-inch thickness, and cut the dough into rectangles or squares about 2 to 3 inches in diameter. At a top corner of the dough, use a straw to poke a hole, remembering that it will shrink a bit when you bake it.

Bake the cookies according to the instructions and let them cool completely. When cool, use tubes of decorator frosting to decorate the cookies. With these tubes, you can add the name of the person to whom each gift will be delivered.

Once you have frosted the cookies, wrap each tightly in plastic wrap and use the straw to poke through the hole in the cookie. Thread a thin piece of ribbon through the hole and attach the cookie name tag to the gift.

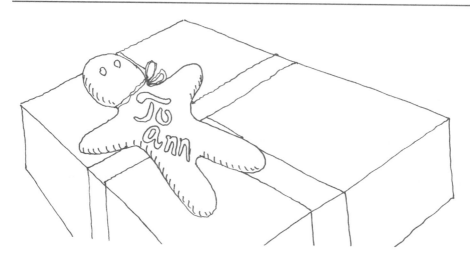

99. Good-night Kissing Rings

You will need: embroidery hoop (one for each child); green and red ribbon or cord; colorful paper; scissors; mistletoe (one piece for each ring)

Many families have a traditional kissing ring somewhere in their house, with a piece of mistletoe in it. Tradition has it that anyone who is caught under the mistletoe needs to be kissed. Why not adapt this tradition and create a good-night kissing ring to hang over each child's bed?

Use an embroidery hoop or other circular object to form the base of the ring. Wrap it with colorful green and red ribbon or cord; then cut paper shapes such as stars, crosses, and hearts, and hang them from the ring with ribbon. Add a piece of mistletoe in the center.

Hang a good-night ring over each child's bed during the month of December as a reminder for a good-night kiss and hug, right in that spot, each night during the month.

SHARE THE JOY OF THE STORY

Although we share the good news of Jesus' birth each day of the year, not just during the Christmas season, it is especially meaningful to share our joy with others at this time. Perhaps that is because other people seem more receptive and willing to share their joy with us during this season.

100. A Family Christmas Carol

Neighborhood Christmas caroling seems to be a thing of the past in many cities today. As people lead busier lives and move about more frequently, they find it harder and harder to really get to know and feel comfortable with their neighbors. Creating a family caroling party is a fun way to share the good news and get to know your neighbors.

Practice a few favorite Christmas carols with your family, and invite other families from your neighborhood or church to join you, if you like. Plan a date when you can go around the neighborhood, singing.

One person I know wanted snow desperately for her caroling party, but it was not to be. Nevertheless, when the group set out to sing, she had snow with her. You see, in her frustration, she decided to make a "snobrella" so that she could carry the snow with her as they went from house to house.

To do this, she cut snowflakes from white tissue paper and attached them to the inside of an old umbrella with clear nylon thread, so that the snowflakes hung down all around her!

If your group of carolers has fun in your neighborhood, think about going to other neighborhoods, or to retirement or nursing homes—why let all that singing practice go to waste!

101. You Can Volunteer

A Sunday afternoon during the month of December is the perfect time to take your family to a place where you can volunteer to help others who are less fortunate. Perhaps a food bank or pantry, or a soup kitchen for people in transitional housing could use your family's help. Maybe a nursing home is in need of someone to help with a worship service or with activities for the residents. Perhaps your church has a special project that could use some extra help during this time of year.

Whatever it is that you and your family might choose to volunteer on a Sunday afternoon, there is nothing like the warm feeling that comes when we, who have been given so much, give some of what we have to others.

> "For I was hungry and you gave me something to eat, I was thirsty and you gave me something to drink, I was a stranger and you invited me in, I needed clothes and you clothed me, I was sick and you looked after me, I was in prison and you came to visit me."
>
> (Matthew 25:35-36)